MOVEMENTS WITH THE COSMIC DANCER

*On the world stage, each individual self is an actor/dancer.
On the Cosmic Plane, Shiva alone is the great Dancer in
Great Time choreographing various scenes in the Great
Universe. This is the journey of an ordinary pilgrim to an
extraordinary place on the Earth.*
*A journey woven with a personal tale of a daughter's search
for her lost father. A tale of a soul longing to dance with the
Movements of the Cosmic Dancer.*

MOVEMENTS WITH THE COSMIC DANCER

On Pilgrimage to Mount Kailash and Lake Manasarovar

LAKSHMI BANDLAMUDI

New Age Books

ISBN: 81-7822-280-9

First Edition: Delhi, 2006

Published by
NEW AGE BOOKS
A-44 Naraina Industrial Area Phase-I
New Delhi-110 028 (INDIA)
Email: nab@vsnl.in
Website: www.newagebooksindia.com

Printed in India at
Nice Printing Press
3, Rashid Market Extension, New Delhi-110 051

Mount Kailash and Lake Manasarovar complement each other in every aspect – the height to its depth, the spirit to its matter, the erotic to the sublime and the immutable to the mutable. Kailash is the all-pervading transcendental God – the *Paramatma* while the lake is the living being – the *Jivatma*, who must find the personal God in the depth of its soul. Like the clear waters of Manasarovar capable of reflecting the Centre of Divinity, the mind must also be clear and become a symbol of fecundity.

Dedicated to my Father
Sri Bandlamudi Visweswariah

this pilgrimage to the abode of the divine father
in heaven is written in fond memory of
my human father on earth.

THE DALAI LAMA

FOREWORD

For many people in south and central Asia, Mount Kailash is the holiest mountain on the earth. In this book Dr. Lakshmi Bandlamudi presents an account of her own pilgrimage to the mountain and nearby Lake Mansarovar.

We Tibetans tend to regard the entire land of Tibet as a realm of Dharma, not only because of the profusion of temples and monasteries, but because we regard even the physical features of the land as sacred. Many pilgrimage sites are associated with great spiritual practitioners. Elsewhere, it is the particular shape of a mountain or curve of a river that provides the indication of positive significance. Mount Kailash possesses both qualities and has long been the object of pilgrims from all over Tibet, as well as from India and beyond. It is sacred to the Bonpos, practitioners of the indigenous pre-Buddhist religion of Tibet. Buddhists associate it with adepts like the great yogi and poet Milarepa and regard it as one of the sacred locations of the meditational deity Heruka. For Hindus it is the abode of the deities Shiva and Parvati, while Jains and Sikhs have their own special associations with it. What is more, even for those without a specific faith, the mountain's physical form and colour makes it a natural symbol of purity.

In the past, Indian pilgrims did not need permits to visit Mount Kailash and Lake Mansarovar; pilgrims had free access to these holy sites as if they were visiting just another part of India. Now both the internal and external situations of Tibet have changed beyond imagination. Therefore, it is heartening to know that in spite of all that has happened, pilgrims from India continue to brave the journey and go to pay their respects at these sacred sites. It continues to be my prayer that all of Tibet becomes a sanctuary, a zone of peace, a place of harmony between people, animals and the environment, treated with the same respect as Mount Kailash and its surroundings. I look forward to the day that the Tibetan people may freely welcome visitors from all over the world to Tibet to share that experience of peace and harmony.

THE DALAI LAMA
December 16, 2005

In Praise of the Book...

Kailash and Manasarovar have occupied a focal point in our spiritual consciousness from the dawn of our civilisation. The magnificent tetrahedron, which stands aloof in majestic splendour, is looked upon as 'the earthly symbol of the mythical Mount Sumeru; the home of the great Lord Shiva, the navel of the world, while the sacred lake is the source of four great rivers that have nourished many civilisations. Numerous books have been written on Kailash and Manasarovar by Indian and foreign authors, but this one by Lakshmi Bandlamudi carries a special ambience as she has woven into it the powerful myth of Lord Shiva as Nataraja, the Cosmic Dancer, a superb symbol of the kinetic Universe in which we find ourselves.

Shiva is surely the most charismatic, mysterious, ambiguous and holistic deity in Hindu pantheon. On the one hand he sits immobile for millennia deep in meditation, surrounded only by the wind and the elements. On the other, he performs the celestial Tandava dance which brings about the creation, preservation and dissolution of the cosmos. The Anand Tandava – the dance of bliss, has been gloriously represented in the Chola Nataraja bronzes and the great Shaiva temple cities of South India. Incidentally, I have had the privilege of building the first Nataraja shrine in North India in the premises of my family Sri Raghunath Temple in Jammu.

Lakshmi Bandlamudi's description of her journey to Manasarovar and Kailash, representing as they do Purusha and Prakriti, the masculine and the feminine nature of existence, is deeply moving because she connects it to her own inner spiritual quest. Replete with mythical stories regarding Shiva and Parvati, and written with a special emphasis on the feminine, this book is a moving testament of a living faith which has persisted for thousands of years. She has also drawn extensively on the writings of the great Kashmir Shaiva Acharya Abhinavagupta and the contemporary Rishi Sri Aurobindo, and this further enriches the text. She has pointed out the great significance of Kailash and Manasarovar for Tibetan Buddhism, and I might add that they are also considered sacred by the two other Indic religions – Jainism and Sikhism.

Ever since I was a child I have been fascinated by Kailash and Manasarovar, and have been enraptured by their photographs, read numerous books about them, so much so that we have named our residence in Delhi *Mansarovar* as it is built around a small pool! I am unlikely to be able to make the pilgrimage myself, but I still cherish the hope that one day I will catch a glimpse of this great mountain from the air. There are already Everest viewing flights from Kathmandu, and if such flights are introduced for Kailash and Manasarovar it would give people the opportunity to have this magnificent darshan from the air. Meanwhile *Movements with the Cosmic Dancer* provides valuable new insights into this great pilgrimage.

Aum namah Shivaya

Taranlingh

Karan Singh

New Delhi
1 June 2005

ACKNOWLEDGEMENTS

✠

My mother is the force behind this book and the pilgrimage and without her encouragement both would not have happened. She lives up to her name – Saraswati, the goddess of knowledge, and the excitement that she shows to any scholarly endeavour is contagious. I must only be ready to lend my attentive ears and she is eager to spill some pearls of wisdom. Her words have allowed me to grow and find strength within.

My wonderful siblings have always given their support to all my eccentric projects. Segment of this book is our collective tale. My sister Usha and my brother-in-law Srinivas show their generosity so readily, even before I ask. My brother Eshwar and my sister-in-law Aarati cannot contain their excitement and they monitor all my travel plans. My youngest brother Raghu makes sure that I have fun. The adorable children in my family—Vinai, Vaman, Adhiti and Maitreyi are the reason for this story. They must know their roots.

My fellow pilgrims have made the journey enjoyable and meaningful.

Advait and Shree not only gave great company during the travel, but also listened to this work patiently as it was progressing, offering their insightful comments. I value their friendship.

Kailas made sure that we were not deprived of tasty snacks during the travel and her husband Indrajit had a calming effect. I thank them for their generosity.

Jyothi always had so many questions about everything and was an attentive listener and her husband Chamraj was very diligent in recording our experiences with all the details. I thank them for sharing their journal and photographs so readily.

The Duvvuri family – Hira and Suri showed their intense devotion to their spiritual Guru and their son Raju entertained us with his singing and chanting. I thank Hira for sharing her photographs.

Last, but not least, Prema was a great travel partner, an accommodating tent-mate, and a spontaneous prayer-mate.

I thank Mr. Aloke C. Bagchi for arranging a great pilgrimage with so much care and attention to details.

I am indebted to our caring and efficient Sherpas – Kinna, Ming Mar, Nimma and Zhangbu. Our Tibetan drivers gave us a safe and jolly ride in an otherwise dangerous terrain with their skill and humour and our Tibetan guide Dadu patiently answered all our queries.

I owe a lot to Jayalakshmi Popuri, my wonderful cousin and a great dialogic partner. I benefited immensely from her bright-red editorial font.

Finally my obeisance to the Universal Parents – Lord Shiva and Goddess Parvati for clearing the path to their abode. They live in my abode and in my heart forever.

PREFACE

Movements with the Cosmic Dancer

These are the movements of an ordinary pilgrim to an extraordinary place on earth. I invite the readers to move back and forth from one plane to another – the physical, spiritual, mythical, philosophical, historical and finally personal. The physical journey is both the story and a backdrop to record the spiritual journey. The tools and the method for spiritual pursuit are drawn from the inexhaustible myths and these myths enable us to understand abstract philosophy and these philosophies are laden with history. The mythical and cultural histories intersect with my personal history. The journey took me to great heights in every sense of the expression only to probe into the depths of my inner being. It is a journey outward and inwards and woven into this multidirectional movement is a personal tale of a daughter's search for her lost father, who had to be reclaimed on a higher plane. Taken together, this multi-layered narrative is the longing of the soul to dance and when the Lord of Dance recognises this desire and extends his helping hand, it transpires into *Movements with the Cosmic Dancer....*

List of Illustrations

1. Svayambhu Nath Stupa in Kathmandu
2. The Scenic Himalayan Terrain
3. The Svayambhu Lingam – a self risen phallic emblem in a cave in Kodari
4. The Majestic Himalayan Range at Kodari near Nepal – Tibet border
5. Ascending through one cloud – layer after another in the mystical Himalayas
6. Gold and Copper coloured hills on the Tibetan Plateau
7. The River Brahmaputra – 'the son of Brahma'. This river was the guide to early explorers
8. Lunch break on the Tibetan Plateau
9. Wading through the flowing streams
10. The first Darshan of Mount Kailash and Lake Manasarovar
11. The Southern face of Kailash. The mountain face is chipped in horizontal lines appearing like the ash marks on Shiiva's forehead
12. The Pilgrim's Path
13. The Yaks carrying the load
14. The 'Ravan Parvat' at the southern face of Kailash
15. The western view of Kailash with broad flat rings appearing like Saturn
16. Footprint of Lord Shiva

CONTENTS

✣

ONE

THE SACRED LANDSCAPE

There is, in the northern quarter, the deity-souled lord of mountains (lit. immovable ones), by name Himalaya (mansion of snow), who stands, like the measuring rod of the earth, spanning (the distance between; lit. having entered) the Eastern and the Western oceans.

Whom having fixed upon as the calf, while mount Meru, clever in milking, stood as the milker, all the mountains milked from the earth (in the shape of a cow), as directed by Prithu, brilliant jewels and great medicinal herbs.

Kalidasa in Kumarasambhava

The Prophesy of Buddha says [most truly],
That this snow mountain is the navel of the world,
A place where the snow leopards dance.
The mountain top, the crystal-like pagoda,
Is the [white and glistening] palace of Dem-Chog.

The great snow mountains which Di Se encircle,
Are the dwelling places of five hundred Arhats.
Here all deities of Eight Divisions pay their homage!
Surrounding it are hills and marshes,
The region abounds with "incense" plants,
The source of nectar-producing drugs.
This is the great place of accomplished yogis;
Here one attains transcendental Samadhis.

> There is no place more wonderful than this,
> There is no place more marvelous than here.
> —*The Hundred Thousand Songs of Milarepa*

This is the tale of a pilgrim's wandering in the mighty Himalayas, more specifically to Mount Kailash – the crown jewel of the Himalayan range and the nearby enchanting Lake Manasarovar in western Tibet. For Hindus, Buddhists, Jains and Bonpos, Kailash is *the* sacred mountain. Standing majestically on a gigantic stage – the Tibetan plateau, this mountain is sacred, mystical and magical. The actor on this stage is none other than the Lord of Dance – Shiva, and every step in his cosmic dance reconfigures the world. For thousands of years sages and saints, explorers and scholars, devotees and demons (in Hindu mythology Shiva is the favourite deity for demons because he sanctions boons with relative ease) have undergone immense hardships to get a glimpse of their creator's residence. Hinduism holds that Kailash is the physical manifestation of the mythical mountain Sumeru – the great mountain at the centre of the universe, and the navel of the earth from which all creation springs forth. Thus, in this region myth and reality, heaven and earth, the creator and the created come face to face, collide, kiss, touch, dance and are eventually transformed. The journey in this rugged terrain is very demanding. The body must be physically fit and the mind must be firm and resolute in its goal to undertake this challenging *Yatra*. The body does not always cooperate; it revolts against the orders that the mind issues. The latter places undue demands on the body and in turn the body begs to recognise its frailty. At that very high altitude, the lungs struggle to take every breath, and the feet strive to take one small step and the hands can barely hold the weight of a walking stick. Only with some divine intervention can one convince the body to endure this arduous task.

Mount Kailash is the navel of the earth, an archetype of the divine centre. It is separated from the surrounding mountain range, making it distinctly an abode of gods. In this region innumerable rocks, water streams and caves have their own legends, and like a Rorschach test of spiritual orientation they appear in different forms in the eyes of the beholder. Each individual responds to this mountain differently, because coming face to face with his creator one has to dig deep into the depths of his soul to seek answers about existence, mortality and liberation.

For Hindus, this mountain is the abode of Shiva and his consort Parvati, —the universal Father and Mother, in charge of destruction and creation. Thus, assembled here are various other deities, fellow gods, the panegyrists, the bards, the jesters, the percussionists, the souls liberated from the cycle of birth and death along with the sentinels of heaven. Here, on the roof of the world – an elevated stage, Shiva is Nataraja, the Lord of Dancers or the King of Actors, and the whole cosmos is his theatre, and the dwellers of the three worlds along with the other gods gather around him to witness the celestial dance and hear the music of the divine choir.

The Buddhists refer to this mountain as Kang Rinpoche, the 'jewel of the snows', and to them this whole region is inhabited by Bodhisattvas – the enlightened ones who have deliberately suspended Nirvana in order to spread Buddha's message of peace and love. Although silent and invisible, their presence can be felt viscerally, a tactile experience of absorbing the spiritual vibrations. This mountain blanketed with snow symbolizes the Buddhist doctrine of white purity and the streams flowing into the lake beneath symbolise one's deliverance to the Realm of the Absolute.

In Jainism, Kailash is known as Mount Ashtapada, and its founder Rishabanatha is said to have achieved spiritual liberation atop the summit.

Before the advent of Buddhism, Tibet's indigenous spiritual tradition was called Bon, and according to Bonpos, their founder Tonpo Shenrab is said to have studied their doctrines in heaven and descended to the mountain top to teach his followers the 'Nine Ways of Bon', and they are on Supreme Doctrine, Prediction, Visual World, Illusion, Existence, Primordial Sound, Tantra, and finally on the code of conduct for the lay follower and the monk. Hence they aptly call this Mount Yung-drung Gu-tzeg – 'Edifice of Nine Swastikas'. To the Bonpos, as to the Hindus, the Swastika is an ancient symbol of power, divinity, permanence and indestructibility. This symbol is practically wedged on the mountain and the deep vertical crevasse can be clearly seen on the southern face.

For a skeptic and an agnostic, Kailash is only a 22,028 feet mountain, relatively smaller than the other peaks in the Himalayan range, although they may very well be dazzled by its architectural grace. The mountain is a perfect tetrahedron, smoothly rounded on the top, giving an impression of a giant dome that can generously offer shelter to those who seek. It is a spectacular conglomerate that stands against the backdrop of its mythical primordial partner – the blue sky. In the eastern side a horizontally stratified conglomerate extends from this mountain, looking exactly like a Shiva *Lingam* in the Hindu temple. Mountaineers or any other experts on geological forms have to be impressed by its comely peak. The adjacent hills and rocks are in perfect proportion and symmetry and seem so meticulously hewed. Hindu texts describe Shiva as *Shilpi*—a sculptor, and wherever he lays his hands they have an artistic touch. While the other taller peaks, particularly Mount Everest can impress one with its sheer overwhelming mass, it cannot boast about its geometrical designs, for its dimensions are roughhewn and its sharp peak pierces crudely into the sky. People are drawn to tall peaks to test their strength against the mountain and experience a sense of conquest, whereas for the faithful the journey to Kailash is made in the spiritual as well as the earthly realm. The pilgrim knows all too well that there is no room for individual glory in this expedition.

Kailash is situated in the Ngari region of Western Tibet, and to reach this highland one has to travel for days in one of the most lonely and desolate regions on earth. Once you ascend through the rugged Himalayan range and get on to the Tibetan plateau, there is hardly any vegetation, and one is confronted with stretches of vast expanse of barren land with varying shades of brown hills and snow peaked mountains criss-crossed by strong winds and flowing streams. By conventional standards, this region may seem to be barren, bleak, and even god-forsaken, but for the pilgrim this is a much sought after exile to experience the godliness of silence in raw nature with all its luminosity and glory. Except for some nomadic herders that you encounter along the way, there is hardly any habitation or access to any cultural inventions or products. Faced with such space and silence, stripped of all the technological accessories, the individual feels superfluous and is forced to take an inward journey. Standing on this earth in its raw elemental form and facing the blue sky that almost seems to close in, the individual must bare his soul in all its naked form and drop all pretensions. While the landscape here seems so unearthly, the sky appears so uncannily touchable. With conventional categories of analysis failing, the individual experiences God as an immediate tangible form in that pure thin cold air.

This region is made doubly sacrosanct by the presence of Lake Manasarovar at the foot of Mount Kailash. Legend has it that this lake was created from the mind—*Manas* of Brahma himself and a dip in this holy lake is said to cleanse one's soul of all its misdeeds. Reflected in its crystal clear water is the image of Kailash, geographically demonstrating the core principle of Hindu philosophy: one must strive to keep the mind like the clear waters of Manasarovar so that divinity can be reflected within the self. This enchanting lake is cradled on the Tibetan plateau at a heavenly altitude of 14,950 feet covering an area of about 200 square miles, with a circumference of about 54 miles and a depth of 300 feet, making it the highest fresh water lake in the world. The beauty of this lake, the taste of its sweet water, its mythical origins and its geographical significance of being the birth place of four majestic rivers have been documented in various scriptures and literary texts. It is said in *Skanda Purana* that the sages who went to the Kailash region to meditate needed sanctified water to drink and bathe and Brahma readily consented to their wish and created the lake as a symbol of fecundity. Thus the text proclaims:

> Whoever touches his body with earth from Manasarovar and bathes in its waters will attain to the paradise of Brahma, and whoever drinks the water will ascend to the heaven of Siva, and even be washed pure from the sins of hundred incarnations, and even the animals which bear the name Manasarovar will enter Brahma's paradise. The water of this lake is like pearls. There are no mountains that can compare to the Himalayas, for in them are Kailas and Manasarovar. As the dew is dried up by the morning sun, so are the sins of men blotted out at the sight of the Himalayas.

Long before the dawn of history and way before any geographer was able to trace the origins of four mighty rivers – Indus, Brahmaputra, Karnali and Sutlej—Hindu scriptures describe Manasarovar as the most beautiful, majestic and fertile lake. Two equally majestic mountains tower over it on both the directions – Gurla Mandatha to the South and Kailash to the North. A panoramic view of this luminous lake between two radiant mountains is one of the most precious jewels that nature can offer – a turquoise set between two diamonds.

All life comes from water. In the beginning there was only water and the primordial sea covered everything. According to *Bhagavatha Purana* Lord Vishnu floated on the cosmic sea for eternity and was unable to perceive any object. Upon realization that his creative powers lay dormant in him, the life forces stirred in him and out of the water's infinite potential all of creation emerged. The cream that was churned from the milky waves of this cosmic sea thickened into the earth and the mountain started rising at the navel of the newborn world. Kailash is the embodiment of that mythical mountain Sumeru. It is the crystallisation of the beginnings of life forms, an immutable and an absolute centre of divinity and the deep blue waters of Manasarovar are the fluid mirror that proudly reflect this creative centre. Encoded in this landscape that juxtaposes the mountain with the lake is a profound symbolic message: the mountain is *Purusha* - the male, the phallic image, while the lake is *Prakriti* – Mother Nature, the changing fluid form. The mountain and the lake are inseparable and they complement each other in every form – the erotic to the sublime, the height to its depth, the spirit to its matter and the immutable to the mutable. If Kailash is the all-pervading transcendental god – the *Paramatma*, the lake is the living being – the *Jivatma*, who must find the personal god in the depth of its soul.

For the Buddhists and the Bonpos alike, the lake and the mountain are the 'mother and father of the earth'; the mountain is the emblem of wise *Dem-Chog*, while the lake symbolizes the compassionate *Ma Pam*. Tibetans call this *Tso Mapham* – 'The Undefeated Lake' or *Tso Rinpoche* – 'The Precious Lake'. The lake is said to be a *Mandala* made of precious gems that give lustre to one's character because its waters fall directly from heaven. In his famous work *The Hundred Thousand Songs*, Milarepa extols the virtues of this lake:

> The fame of Ma Pam Lake is indeed far-spreading;
> People say of it in distant places,
> "Ma Pam is like a green-gemmed Mandala!"
> When one approaches closer,
> One sees there waters [cold and] plentiful.

As prophesied by the Buddha in past ages,
This lake is called "The Lake-That's-Never-Warm,"
The fountainhead of four great rivers,
A place where fish and otters swim.

The four great rivers that originate from this lake are the Brahmaputra, the Indus, the Sutlej and the Karnali. Tibetans refer to Brahmaputra as *Tamchog-Khambab* – 'the river flowing out of a horse's mouth' in the West; the Sutlej *Langche-Khambab* — 'the river flowing out of the elephant's mouth' in the South; the Indus as *Senge-Khambab* – 'the river flowing out of a lion's mouth' in the East and the Karnali as *Magcha-Khambab* – 'the river flowing out of a peacock's mouth' in the North. These four animals facing four directions are said to be the symbolic vehicles of The Buddha and therefore parts of the universal Mandala, of which Kailash is the centre.

Hindu scriptures also have their own legends about these rivers. Once upon a time, King Bhagiratha did severe penance to request Ganga to descend to earth and redeem his ancestors who had been reduced to ashes and denied entry to heaven due to a curse by Sage Kapila. As Ganga responds to this call and begins her descent, Gods fearing that her irrepressible nature could deluge the world appeal to Lord Shiva to intervene. Shiva – the most virile of all men contains her force and arrests her in his matted hair. He then loosens the knot gently and releases her tributaries in four different directions. These are the four mighty rivers that travel great distances and make vast portions of South East Asia fertile. Both Hindu and Buddhist scriptures claim, which incidentally have been confirmed by various geographers and explorers, that these rivers encircle the Kailas-Manasarovar region

seven times before flowing in various directions. It is
the dance of the rivers – an homage to the parent lake
and mountain before venturing out in the world. These
are some of the longest rivers in the world that travel
great distances before merging into the sea.

The lake Manasarovar is shaped like the Sun; 'Manas'
in Sanskrit means mind, and thus the lake symbolises
forces of light, consciousness and enlightenment. At a
distance of about 2 to 5 miles and at an altitude 500 feet
lower than Manasarovar is another large lake called
Rakhshas Tal or Rakhshas Sarovar. 'Rakhshas' in
Sanskrit means demon and this lake shaped like a
crescent moon represents the dark, unconscious and
demonic forces. The famous demon king Ravana of
Lanka is said to have done penance in this region and
with his muscle power was even able to lift Mount
Kailash. When Lord Shiva applied pressure from the
top, his hands were pressed and to appease Shiva,
Ravana sang a hymn describing the splendour of the
cosmic dance. Therefore, while Manasarovar
symbolises wisdom and calmness, Rakhshas Tal
represents base instincts and chaos. Tibetans call this
Langak Tso – 'a lake in which five mountains are
drowned'. Figuratively speaking, it is a brute force
capable of devouring anything. If Manasarovar elevates
consciousness, Rakhshas Tal has the capability of
engulfing it. The co-existence of these two lakes seems
epiphenomenal; the birth process of anything sacred
and beautiful is accompanied by its converse – the
profane and the ugly. The ugliness is not at the surface
level, in fact both Manasarovar and Rakhshas Tal are
equally beautiful to look at, but their temperament,
taste and size are very different. The circumference of

Rakhshas Tal is about 77 miles compared to Manasarovar's 54 miles, emblematic of the predicament of human existence. The dark demonic forces outweigh the bright forces of wisdom. Manasarovar is a fresh water lake and hence its waters taste absolutely sweet, whereas Rakhshas Tal is a salt-water lake and contains more hard minerals, thus making it less suitable for consumption. Although these two lakes are practically next door neighbours, their personalities are distinctly different. While the waves in Manasarovar are gentle and even, Rakhshas Tal has high roaring waves that are turbulent and tempestuous. There is a geological explanation for this: while Manasarovar is enclosed by two tall peaks – Gurla Mandhata to the South and Kailash to the North, Rakhshas Tal is left exposed in its southern shore. With no mountain on one side to take the southern winds, Rakhshas Tal becomes stormy and rough. These lakes are separated; however on rare occasions the swollen waters from Manasarovar may flow into Rakhshas Tal and when this happens it is considered to be an auspicious event by Tibetans – a blessing from heaven—a helping hand from above to do the cleansing act.

The two lakes along with the mountain symbolise the eternal truth – a formula for human aspiration in the earthly life. The mountain etched with a symbol of Swastika signifying eternal creativeness presides over the two lakes – the Rakhshas Tal to the left in the form of a crescent, symbolising terrifying darkness, ignorance and fiendishness, and to its right, at a higher altitude is the round shaped Manasarovar depicting solar forces, piety and enlightenment. In this sacred space, a timeless truth is carved out: the human being must strive to rise from darkness and nescience to brightness and knowledge and eventually blend in with the Brahman – the Universal Being. The mountain with its divine vision and roving perspective bears witness to and takes stock of human misdeeds and meritorious acts and maintains an accurate account of its assets and liabilities.

Along the shoreline of Manasarovar there were eight monasteries as documented by the unquestioned authority on this region, Swami Pranavananda who between 1928 and 1949 made 25 circuits of the mountain and 23 of the lake and gave a detailed account of the physiography of this region. According to this mendicant-explorer, the eight monasteries around Lake Manasarovar were, (1) Gossul Gompa (West), (2) Chiu Gompa (North West), (3) Cherkip Gompa (North), (4) Langpona Gompa (North), (5) Ponri Gompa (North), (6) Seralung Gompa (East), (7) Yerngo Gompa (South), and (8) Thugolho Gompa (South), whereas only one monastery – Chepgey Gompa near Rakhshas Tal at its north-western corner was recorded by Swami Pranavananda. To build a monastery around Rakhshas Tal and reside in it is to absorb even more demonic energy, whereas to stay and meditate around Manasarovar is to breathe in freshness and purity and experience tranquility. Almost all of these monasteries were destroyed during the Cultural Revolution, and even those that survived are in a dilapidated state. Only in recent years some of them are being renovated and reconstructed with donations from pilgrims. As always Tibetans firmly believe that Cultural Revolutions and political forces can only bring down structures but cannot erase the sanctity of this place. Only the monasteries are built by human effort but the shrine here is a gift of nature and no oppressive regime can sully or demolish this sacred landscape. Herein lies the liberating spirit of the Tibetan soul.

Since time immemorial Himalayas (abode of snow) have been elevated to great spiritual heights, the great ice-wall crowning the Indian sub-continent, stretching close to 1600 miles and covering 200 to 300 miles in breadth, is truly on a super-human scale, at once dazzling and dangerous. Humans may go to this region to test their strength, but their senses clearly instruct them to genuflect. Hindu scripture, classical poetry, modern literature, mountaineers and explorers from every part of the world have written in praise of these snow- clad mountains. The great Sanskrit poet Kalidasa described the Himalayas as the 'measuring rod of the earth', unparalleled in its majesty and beauty. Scattered throughout are a variety of rich minerals and medicinal herbs, adding pleasant fragrance to the clean air. In Kalidasa's description of the Kailas-Manasarovar region in his classic work *Kumarasambhava*, the rich metals appear like an 'untimely twilight' as their colours reflect in patches of cloud, and the phosphorescent herbs shed light into the deep interior of caves, and the clouds hanging over the entrances to caverns serve as a screen to scantily clothed celestial lovers in an amorous mood. The wind here fills up the holes in bamboo trees producing melodious music to which the peacocks dance, and the Yogis who come here to witness this splendour are sprayed with waters of Ganges by the Wind–God as a welcoming gesture. Hindu scriptures describe the entire Himalayan range as an embodiment of the divine; its inaccessible and cloud-wrapped peaks are the abode of gods. Tucked in these mountains are innumerable shrines of Shiva, but his Principal abode is in Kailas. Texts present varying images of Shiva in Kailas, ranging from a naked ash-smeared ascetic in deep meditation to the romantic partner with his wife Parvati on his lap to the responsible family man with his wife and two sons watching over his earthly children.

It is customary for Hindus and Buddhists to do *Parikrama* of (circumambulate) any divine symbol in a clock-wise direction. Although Mount Kailash is separated from the main Himalayan range, other smaller mountains, hills and rocks all having some symbolic meaning are connected to it. Thus, the whole region referred to as *Shiva-Loka* (world of Shiva) is approximately 32 miles in circumference and it takes three days to complete one circuit. Most pilgrims manage to do one circuit provided the weather conditions are favourable. Unpredictable rains and blizzards often place a damper on the determined sojourner. The circuit path is extremely rugged, and the wayfarer ascends from an altitude of 14,500 feet to 19,500 feet reaching the famed Dolma La Pass on the second day. Some orthodox Buddhists do what is called *sashtanga-danda-pradakshina* (total body prostration circuit) of the Kailash and some complete the circuit in one day called *ningkor*. Today many Tibetans, mostly dissidents undertake the one-day circuit to escape Chinese authorities and rush back to their exiled countries.

The ritual of *Parikrama* (circling a divine symbol) has special meaning to Hindus and Buddhists, as it gives them a unique view from each angle. The belief is that the Universal Divine Being manifests in many forms and each believer prefers a different path or a different form of the divine. By circling the divine symbol the devotee recognises the multifarious forms of the divine being, and the multiple paths that fellow believers take, and salutes to various incarnations of the divine and the different routes that each individual takes. While circling, each point gives a different view and each is splendid in its own right and no single point can claim superiority over the other but what is significant is that in a circle any point is equidistant from the centre.

In Buddhist and Hindu temples there is always a flag-staff emblematic of the shrine, and in the western side of the Mount Kailash there is a big flag-staff called *Tarboche* (*Tar* means flag and *che* means big) and as is the custom, pilgrims circle this flag-staff as they proceed with their *Parikrama*, as a show of reverence. There are five Buddhist monasteries around Mount Kailash: (1) Nyanri Gompa (West), (2) Dira-phuk Gompa (North), (3) Zuthul-phuk Gompa (East), (4) Gengta Gompa (South), and (5) Silung Gompa (South). While circling the mountain, one comes across huge *Shapjes* – foot prints of Shiva/Buddha in four different places. In every Hindu temple, in the southwest corner it is customary to install the idol of Ganesha, the god who confers boons and removes all obstacles, and in the south west corner of Mount Kailash one encounters a huge elephant shaped rock. Thus, evident in this nature's shrine is every architectural detail of a temple.

To the western world Kailash-Manasarovar has remained elusive until the eighteenth century, when the first known European, an Italian Jesuit missionary – Father Ippolito Desideri—ventured out into this region and recorded his voyage in his landmark book 'An Account of Tibet'. Desideri travelled all across India and Tibet between 1712 – 1727 and sometime in 1715 he traversed from eastern to western Tibet guided by the river Brahmaputra and he described Kailash as "a mountain of excessive height and great circumference, always enveloped in clouds, covered with snow and ice, and most horrible, barren, steep and bitterly cold" (p83).* In the same region he reported spotting the cave where 'Urghien' – Padmasambhava, the patron saint who brought Tantric Buddhism into Tibet from India, is said to have meditated. Father Desideri undertook this voyage with the blessings of Pope Clement XI to detect if there were any Christian communities sheltered in the Himalayas and to revive the evangelisation of this region.

Almost a century later, Europeans who dared into this region were mostly explorers who were keen on solving a geographic riddle. They wanted to trace the origins of four great rivers of India in order to support or refute the claims of Hindu texts that placed their genesis to Lake Manasarovar and to draw an accurate world map. Official maps until this time had shown Tibet as a huge gaping hole covered with snow. In 1812 William Moorcroft, a British veterinarian journeyed into the Tibetan frontier as part of a scouting expedition by the East India Company and discovered Manasarovar, but was eventually found murdered in Tibet. In much of the mid-19th century Tibet closed its frontiers with India, making it difficult for official cartographers to venture out into this region. The high altitude, extreme and unpredictable weather conditions along with murderous tribes posed risk at every step.

---

* See Ippolito Desideri (1937) *An Account of Tibet – The Travels of Ippolito Desideri,* 1712-1727.

In the early part of the 20th century, at the height of western imperialism, there were other interests that led Europeans into this region. The most notable one was when Sir Francis Younghusband with his British troops in 1904 marched into Lhasa in an attempt to beat the Russians in the dirty race to colonise. Equipped with all the ammunition of the British army, it didn't take long for Younghusband's expedition to wipe out the Tibetan army. It was a classic battle between the guns and the Mantras, and even before the Tibetan army could fully surrender to the British might, Younghusband found himself drawn to the protective talismans and their mystical chantings. The British withdrew after signing trade agreements and Younghusband became a mystic and spent the rest of his life singing the glory of the Himalayas.

The first known westerner to follow the pilgrim's path around Kailash was the Swedish explorer Sven Hedin, who after studying geography in Berlin, set out to trace the source of the four great rivers of India and wrote a three volume travelogue 'Trans-Himalaya'. Although he succeeded in solving the mystery of the four rivers – the Indus, the Sutlej, the Brahmaputra and the Karnali, his account received heavy criticism from the British Royal Geographical Society for inaccuracies and exaggerations and eventually was expelled from the society for his Nazi connections. Sven Hedin's erroneous claims were later corrected by Swami Pranavananda, an explorer and mendicant who made several circuits around the mountain and sounded the lakes and gave the most comprehensive account of this region in his famous book 'Kailas-Manasarovar', filled with scientific and spiritual observations.

The most esoteric account of this region came from the German Buddhist monk Lama Anagarika Govinda about his pilgrimage to Kailash in 1948 who wrote his reflections in his famous book *'The Way of the White Clouds'*. For him the pilgrimage itself was emblematic of the white summer-cloud, that is so carefree and in harmony with heaven and earth and goes wherever the wind takes it. In the same way the pilgrim also surrenders to the earth below and the sky above and the white clouds that come in between and goes into the depth of her being to clear the inner cloud and reach the farthest horizons of the inner soul. The pilgrim here is at the mercy of the cloud – it can either clear the path to give a bright view of the mountain and not interfere with the journey or it can envelop the mountain and pour torrential rain and prevent the *Darshan* and make the journey hazardous. The image of the free-roaming cloud is frequently invoked in Sanskrit and Buddhist literature; it is the *Dharma-Megha* – 'the cloud of the Universal Law', the *Kala-Megha* – 'the cloud of Time', that set events in motion, the *Megha-Duta* – 'the cloud messenger', which by being in the middle filters and conveys messages between earthly beings and heavenly gods. The external cloud is only a metaphor to draw attention to the clouded mind that needs to be cleared in the pilgrimage. In the great epic Mahabharath, there is a whole section called *Tirtha-yatra Parva* – a 'section on pilgrimage' in the third Canto, *Vana Parva* that extols the merits of pilgrimage, which come not from the actual physical journey, but from the inner journey that is 'holy, entertaining and sanctifying'. The hardships, the uncertainties and the eventual delight that one experiences become a symbol for life.

Since time immemorial determined pilgrims have tried to overcome personal inadequacies and natural calamities to undertake this *Yatra*. They were simply impelled by strong faith, but that ritual came to a halt in 1950 when the Chinese army entered Tibet. After the Indo-China war in 1959 the pilgrimage route from India was closed, and in the years that followed with the Cultural Revolution of China, every aspect of Tibetan life and Buddhist religion came under attack. Prominent monks were exiled into India and other parts of the world and reasonable people were driven into the mountains to lead a desperate life of guerrillas, their monuments and monasteries were demolished, their statues smashed, books made into bonfire—in short every aspect of their cultural life repressed. There is an Indian adage that says even if God gives the boon, the priest withholds it, and nowhere is it expressed more clearly as in the case of the Chinese Red Guard attacking the very roots of Tibetan identity. China's policy on Tibet began to relax since 1980 giving greater degree of religious freedom. In 1981 the governments of India and China reached a special agreement and the pilgrimage route was reopened. Although there are still restrictions on the number of pilgrims who are allowed to enter this region each year, the path has been cleared, at least officially, even though many pilgrims routinely complain of being interrogated and harassed for variety of unexplained reasons.

Cultural revolutions and oppressive regimes can only tear down man-made structures, but the sanctity of this region is beyond any human interference. When the pilgrim experiences the spiritual vibrations emanating from this region, its sacredness is further enhanced in the human consciousness, and these feelings again and again reconfirm the tales congealed in the past. Mountains, rivers and lakes that are imbued with myths and tales never had any beginning, they are always holy and majestic, but when humans discover them a transformation occurs in their consciousness. When that happens a mountain is no longer just a mountain, it is elevated to great symbolic heights that make the human spirit soar. A heightened consciousness does elevate a mountain. Mount Kailash is indeed raised from an earthly peak into the realm of divine by the faithful, giving further credence to the timeless myths. The pilgrims do not believe that it is up to them to make plans to go into this region, the call must come and the path must be cleared, and I yearned for that call to take part in this spatio-temporal wonderment.

TWO

THE DANCE OF THE SOUL

Sadamchita- mudamchita – nikunchita – padam Jhalajhala –
cchalita – manju - katakam
Patanjali driganjana – mananjana – achanchala – padam
janana bhanjanakaram
Kadambarchi – mambaravasam parama – mambuda-
vidambaka – galam
Chidambuda- manim budha hridambuja – ravim para –
chidambaranatam hridi bhaje   1

Sambhu Natanam by Patanjali.
Translation and Commentary by H.H. Swamini Sarada
Priyananda. Chinmayaranyam

Adore in the heart of the supreme Dancer of Chidambaram,
whose foot is well moving, lifted and bent. His beautiful
bracelets move making the *jhala jhala* sounds. It is *Anjana* (a
special collyrium applied to eyes to see the hidden treasures buried in the ground) to the eyes of Patanjali. It is without a blemish. It is the motionless Abode. It is capable of
breaking the wheel of births. He has the glow of red *Kadamba*
flowers and is skyclad. He is the Supreme. His neck defeats
the darkness of a cluster of rain clouds. He is the shining
diamond of clouds of consciousness. He is the Sun to the
lotus of the hearts of wise people.

Nietzsche, one of my favourite philosophers, declared
in his Zarathustra's speeches that one "should believe

only in a god who understood how to dance." The image of a dancing god is all too familiar to me, but the thought of my relationship with my creator as a dance seems even more exhilarating. Having sanctioned the 'will to power' and the 'will to choose', the creator perhaps expects the humans to take 'steps' and dance with him. After all, humans are not inert beings thrown into this world whose steps are entirely orchestrated by the divine being; instead the mortal beings must strive to take thoughtful steps and recognise their wrongful steps. One cannot take steps with impunity, and god cannot be an alibi for all the spurious moves that one makes. To assume that every step that we take is orchestrated by divine force would mean assigning the role of a puppeteer to the creator, rendering the subjects as passive puppets. Nietzsche abhors such a consciousness as the 'religious view' of a 'camel', that feels imprisoned and is only a recipient of given values and stoically endures the hardships inflicted upon it by the world. The great Indian thinker, Sri Aurobindo who has given the most comprehensive exposition on the 'Integral Yoga', refers to such a consciousness as a *Tamasic* surrender, where the individual says, "I won't take any steps, let God do everything." Here inertia, dullness and an inability to regenerate vital forces and reevaluate their standard formula and routine actions mark the consciousness. On the other hand to affirm that we alone are responsible for every movement is to devalue the greater force which Nietzsche describes as the consciousness of a lion that establishes its supremacy by terrorizing the world. Sri Aurobindo also cautions against relying solely on one's own efforts,

---

Thus Spoke Zarathustra, Of Reading and Writing.

because when faced with adversities the consciousness either disintegrates or falsely affirms itself with brute power. While the consciousness of a camel is passively nihilistic, the lion embodies reactive nihilism and neither is suited for a good dance. Instead one must be actively nihilistic, like a child who boldly takes steps, even while receiving adult guidance. The child's play embraces innocence and persistence in the act with the knowledge of a greater force and yet possesses a prophetic awareness of a potential fall. The child is always so seriously playful, and Nietzsche avers that the creator favours this kind of play seeking companions in the dance and not "corpses or herds or believers". The childlike play is the true nature of a *Sadhak* – the spiritual aspirant, says Sri Aurobindo for it is based on a certain relative free will even while surrendering to the Divine force. The creator rejoices in that 'childlike' dance with his subjects since it has innumerable acts. At times they could synchronise their steps to a harmonious rhythm, and sometimes they may create ruptures to establish their unique identities, and at other times they may pay homage and surrender or playfully tease and mock each other. Like the matted locks of Shiva's hair that move so gracefully in his cosmic dance, imagination springs forth in this childlike dance on earth—so sublime a metaphor to depict the unity of *Paramatma* and *Jivatma*.

The clearest image of dance as primary activity of god is epitomised by the Lord of Kailash; he is Nataraja – the Lord of Dance and his cosmic dance awakens the inert nature in all living beings, penetrating them with pulsing waves of primeval sound – the *Omkara*. The earthly beings who have been caught up in a somnambulist whirl are now drawn into the 'Immortal Rhythms of the Great Dance', and in the fullness of time and space the cosmic dancer rejoices in the small steps that his subjects take. The Lord of Dance like the latent heat in firewood that simply cannot contain it within itself, but will diffuse it into dry wood, is always eager to diffuse his power and talent to his creation so that they can also partake in the dance. When Shiva – the *Purusha* (spirit, individual soul) begins his dance, the *Prakriti* along with the whole cosmos is awakened and in this primeval dance one sees the choral dancing of his subjects and the planetary constellations, harmoniously interweaving and interchanging.

It is this kind of dance that Nietzsche was seeking with his creator and like his Zarathustra, I too pleaded with my creator, " I dance after you, I follow you even when only the slightest traces of you linger. Where are you? Give me your hand! Or just a finger!"*

Ever since the desire to go to Kailash lodged in my mind, I have been making this earnest plea to Lord Shiva. I can only file a petition, but the call must come from Him and the path cleared by Him. Will he extend his finger? My soul longs for that dance, just that one small step with the cosmic dancer. If that father of mine can extend just his pinky finger and take one small step, my consciousness will soar by leaps and bounds. Nietzsche says that the 'dancer wears his ears in his toes' and my heels and toes were all 'ears' ready to join the caravan of pilgrims. Just the mere aspiration itself raised my heels and my feet were already 'tossing in a mad dance' in innumerable imaginary trips to Kailash.

---

* Thus Spoke Zarathustra, *The Second Dance*, p, 241. Translation: R.J. Hollingdale.

If my ears go to my toes how will I hear the call? Even if my ears are in their place, do I have the capacity to hear? There was no point in worrying over these matters. If the call comes, the creator will provide the mechanism to hear. It is not within my comprehension as to what kind of game the Lord of Dance is going to play. In fact it is the surprise, the playfulness, the *Lila* that makes the dance so enchanting and exciting. Zarathustra says to his redeemer, "At my feet, my dancing mad feet, you throw a glance, a laughing, questioning, melting tossing glance:" and then the dance began. It is a game of 'hide and seek' filled with creativity, illusion, surrender and liberation, and that's what the cosmic dance is all about.

The dance of Shiva represents the five syllables in his name *Na Ma Si Va Ya* and these syllables maintain balance in the five elements that comprise the universe – space, air, fire, earth and water. The dance is the manifestation of his five fold activity (*Panchakritya)*, namely, Creation (*Srishti*), Preservation (*Sthithi*), Destruction (*Samhara*), Illusion (*Tirobhava*) and finally Salvation (*Anugraha*). It is said that Nataraja has been engaged in the Dance of Bliss (*Ananda Tandava*) ever since the inception of the universe, and his dance posture is an emblem of these activities. The dance always takes place within an arch of flames, and of his four arms, one right arm holds the drum announcing every creative act, and the other right hand is held up signaling protection. One of his left arms holds a ball of fire needed to annihilate dark forces and his other left arm points to his raised left foot that liberates individuals from cycles of birth and death. His right foot stands on a crouching figure of a demon that must be released from the snares of illusion and ignorance.

Dance is a complete art form that engages the whole body and soul and incorporates all other art forms; a perfect symbol of *Advaita* – the philosophy of non-dualism, making no distinctions between matter and spirit, God and human. It is an aesthetic delight; pleasing to our senses and fulfilling to our mind as it integrates every other art form. Dance is the crown jewel in the pavilion of drama as it gives finest expression to ornate lyrics set to melodious music through gross and subtle body movements. As the Lord of this complete art form, Shiva cannot contain his delight within himself, but must pour out this wonder into his multifarious manifestations. Dance is not just his activity, but it is the very nature of his relationship with his subjects. This is the cosmic dance that imparts the science to his subjects, transforms them and eventually absorbs them back into the Universal Being. Like the spider that spins the cobweb from itself, dwells in it and is again capable of drawing it into itself, the cosmic dancer transmits his art and energy into his creation, rejoices in the wonderment and sanctions salvation to the worthy subjects.

Why is dance symbolic of the creator? What is it that I can know about dance through the Divine Being or what do I know about the Divine Being through dance? I find the most plausible explanation in *Mundakopanishad* in which *Saunaka*, a householder interested in understanding the science of the Spirit approached *Angiras* and questioned, 'What is that, knowing which everything in the world becomes known?" To this fundamental question encompassing all sciences and philosophy, *Angiras* explained that by knowing the Supreme, one understands the meaning of all existence.

That is because the creation originates from Brahman and dissolves into it almost effortlessly, just as the spider spins the cobweb out of its own abdomen and again draws it into itself with perfect ease. *Angiras* further explained that the goal is to achieve two kinds of knowledge – one the lower kind that consists of concrete subject-matter like the Vedas, the code of rituals, grammar, etymology and so on, and the other higher knowledge which is abstract and concerned with the nature of the Brahman that is invisible, ungraspable, eternal, all pervading and immeasurably subtle. Analogously, dance incorporates every other art form, making an earthly performance so ethereal. It is at once a hard core science and fine art. Therefore, the cosmic dance must be understood on several planes and its deepest significance is felt when it is realised that it takes place within each soul. About this sacred dance, the great devotee of Lord Shiva, Tirumoolar instructs to his fellow devotees,

> The dancing foot, the sound of the tinkling bells,
> The songs that are sung and the varying steps,
> The form assumed by our Dancing *Gururpura*—
> Find out these within yourself, then shall your
> fetters fall away.
>
> *(Periya Puranam)*

To this end dance must not be understood literally, but as an attempt to rid ourselves of the fetters that bind us preventing a free, joyous dance. In fact the cosmic dance of Lord Shiva performed in the ecstasy of joy is not visible when deluded, but once we drop all pretensions the divine dance becomes an eye-opener giving a new vision of the cosmic play. The deepest significance is felt when one realises that it takes place within each soul, and this point is made succinctly by the Lord of Dance himself in *Shiva-Sutras*. Legend has it that Shiva revealed profound aphorisms to Vasugupta in the Mahadeva Mountain in the Kashmir valley and they came to be known as *Shiva-Sutras* forming the backbone of Kashmir *Saivism*.

One of the aphorisms says, '*Nartaka Atma*' – The Self is the Dancer (*Shiva-Sutras*, 3.9). On the world stage each individual Self is an actor/dancer. On the Cosmic plane, Shiva alone is the Great Dancer in Great Time, choreographing various scenes in this Great Universe. When the whole world is asleep only Shiva, the producer of the world-drama is awake, because Shiva is the supreme universal consciousness that willfully contracts and descends to become the individual consciousness. However the individual does not recognise this truth readily due to ignorance, delusion and limitations of the mind. The remedy for this obtuseness, according to the Kashmir Saiva philosophical system is *Pratyabhijna* – recognition of the fact that the individual self is part of the divine and through spiritual discipline one can attain 'at-one-ment' with the supreme. The cosmic dancer dwelling in the souls of individuals makes them dance.

Why is the actor/dancer emblematic of an evolved soul? Is our existence on earth a mere pretense and is our role on the world stage a theatrical performance for entertainment? This is indeed not the case as *Natya* (dance) is born out of four Vedas and their ancillaries, and it is bound by rules and regulations, and hence called *Natya Sastra*. Besides, the pavilion of dance/drama is guarded by innumerable gods. Thus our act on this earth is not a matter of light amusement, wearing an assortment of masks and deceiving fellow actors and spectators, and negating the seriousness of the play. After all, the creator does not recommend that we live like ungrateful guests on earth, even while benefiting from the generosity of Mother Nature and enjoying the hospitality of fellow beings. Such an existence is human, all too human with no traces of divinity. Life sunk deep in untruth (act, pretense) can only be filled with reckless negation, despair and scorn, whereas, the evolved soul, like a talented actor plays the role with utmost serious- ness, honouring the stage and the audience. One is in it and yet not in it, like the water droplet on a lotus leaf.

The source of any fine drama is *Maya* – Illusion, and the actors who play many roles are both in it and above. Without the detachment there can be no aesthetic distance and subsequently no great acting or drama can take place. The individual Self must fully engage the *Maya* – Illusion—and yet transcend it to become fully aware of its inner subtle nature. Thus, the costumes that we don, the dialogues that we deliver, and the roles that we play are all enacted within the inner self, as the *Shiva-Sutras* (3:10) proclaim *Rango antaratma* – 'The inner Self is the stage'. And on this inner stage all masks are peeled off leaving no room for deception. We cannot fool ourselves, because as the next *Shiva-Sutra* (3:11) says, *Preksakani Indriyani* – 'The senses are the spectators.' For both the outer and the inner drama, our sense organs are the spectators and true judges. When the vision is directed inwards, one realises that the inner drama/dance is nothing but a microcosm of the cosmic drama/dance. With that Self-Realisation, the distinction between the individual self and the Universal Self is dissolved and when these curtains drop, one becomes a true Yogi, who is capable of recognising the subtle inner throb in his 'hall of consciousnes'. That is why it is said that the Dance of Bliss takes place in *Cidambaram* – 'sky of consciousness'—and the supreme intelligence dances in the soul to keep the body and the mind from fluctuations, and that is true Yoga. That is why the Lord of Dance is also the Lord of Yoga who instructs us on perfecting both the body and the mind for aesthetic delight and inner peace.

Paradox is the power of the cosmic dancer; the god who can sit still in static trance can with great ease twist and turn in ecstatic dance, achieving perfection both in stillness and movement. This god inspires so much awe as he represents both a resolution and assimilation of paradoxes, and that is why even the gods who witness his dance tremble with devotion, at once experiencing love, fear, wonderment, anxiousness, surrender and hope. It is said in *Shiva Mahimnah Stotra* (Praises to the glory of Shiva):

> You dance for the redemption of the universe
> Yet the earth fears it will crack
> At once beneath the pounding of your feet,
> Yet the star-studded sky fears the peril of the
> flailing of your arms,
> As fierce as iron bars;
> Yet the heavens whipped by waving locks of your
> matted hair,
> Trembles too,
> Your great power is perverse indeed.

In the mythologies of Shiva, his personality is full of ambiguities, simultaneously idealising passion and renunciation, eroticism and asceticism, compassion and rage. He is a faithful husband and a vagrant lover. He is the one who protects the world and liberates the individual from the world, and, wielding his trident, is also capable of its destruction. His personality never ceases to amaze and intrigue, and undoubtedly that's the reason the mountain that Shiva resides in has constantly beckoned pilgrims. Lama Anagarika Govinda rightly said, "There are mountains which are just mountains and there are mountains with personality." Mount Kailash is neither the tallest mountain nor is it a sportive mountain, yet people are drawn to it and are willing to undergo any amount of hardship and privation to get a glimpse of this sacred mountain. To appreciate the multifaceted personality of this mountain and its resident, Lama Govinda recommends that we see the mountain from a distance and in close proximity at various hours of the day in different seasons to gain a deeper understanding of human life that is so intense and varied. After all, every tale about Shiva points to this many-sidedness of his personality.

The Magic of the Story and the Glory of the Hero

A story is the simplest vehicle of truth; it allows us to make sense of ourselves and the world around us. Whether we are trying to solve a moral dilemma, or understand a complex human relationship or are eager to pull ourselves away from a sticky problem, or pursue a deep philosophical question, we just enter the mythical field and we are likely to find a path, a suggestion or an answer. For an Indian 'storying' is just a way of living. Like the children spinning tops in the street corner, the grown-ups in a typical Indian household are always spinning tales enticing listeners and other playmates into this wonderful game of story telling. It is indeed a game, a dance so serious and yet so playful. The narrative pull is so strong; it is better to yield as there is much to be gained. My household was no different. My *Avva*—grandmother was a master storyteller. Growing up in the hot and humid city of Madras, the most memorable part of my childhood was my *Avva* regaling us with tales from the epics – narrating and enacting various plots as we slept in the open-air terrace. These tales of love, sacrifice, deception and abduction were enough to stir one's imagination. Against the backdrop of a cool summer breeze filled with the fragrance of jasmine flowers, imagination and curiosity would burgeon as I gaped into the star-lit sky pondering about rights and responsibilities, *Karma* and *Dharma,* and predicaments of womanhood. *Avva* always reminded us that these epic characters were not living beyond the sky or in a book, but were walking in the streets of India or for that matter in any part of the world. Wisdom lies in detecting them amongst us. Stories were not restricted only to the bedtime: they were told anytime, whenever there was a discussion be it a family matter, a social problem, a political crisis or when you had time to idle. They were inserted into any talk, at joyous occasions or tragic events or during plain gossip. Very often, I could not figure out when the epic tale ended and when the family tale began. They just seemed so seamless. The speed with which the mind went back and forth from the immediate present into the timeless past I thought, could put any modern-day space shuttle to shame. If there is a thought then a story must be told. Otherwise the stomach would simply bulge and burst. This was my ontological reality.

Stories were further reinforced from other sources. In a cultural city like Madras, there was no scarcity of entertainment in the form of classical dance, folk drama in the streets, serious drama in the theatre, religious discourse in the temples in addition to the quintessential Indian obsession the movies. When one imbibes these tales with such frequency and intensity, characters like Rama, Krishna and Shiva are not remote figures who reside in the temples, but imaginary friends who share your secrets. There was no need to penetrate the metaphysical flimflam or be bamboozled by philosophical debates to gain familiarity with these characters. The stories brought them very close to your heart.

A character that embodies all aspects of creation and every human emotion does linger in your heart forever. There is nothing that is negated by the Lord of Kailash. All life forces are grouped together, skillfully orchestrated such that everything has its place, every being has its function, and all participate in the divine concert and their very dissonance creates the most beautiful harmony. Spiritual purity and sensual joy, hideous demonic energy and sublime calmness coexist to produce the true rhythm of life. These ambiguities and paradoxes in Shiva's character do inspire laughter. In fact, he is the laughing god as one of his epithets is *Attahasa* – 'boisterously laughing god', and he is also the god who is laughed at as he is the '*Bhola Shanker*' – 'the gullible one'. To all the seekers of his boons he sanctions them with complete ease without ever suspecting their sinister motives. It is not his nature to send anyone away empty handed when approached. This naivete also puts him into trouble and Vishnu—

the other god in the pantheon, who is the lord of illusion, must often bail him out. Like an embarrassed child of an eccentric and credulous parent one feels like shielding such irrepressible actions and these anecdotes produce laughter. While Shiva is boisterous, impetuous and gullible, Vishnu is calm, measured and critical. They both represent two sides of the comic coin – the fool and the trickster, and affirm the power of laughter. After all laughter exposes truth in all it's naked and changing form and thus getting the joke is a sign of intellect and wisdom. That is why it is said in *Chandogya Upanishad* (3.17.3), "When one laughs, eats and makes love, he joins in the sacrificial chant and recitation." Of all the human sentiments, laughter alone has the capacity to penetrate the depths of meaning, challenge superficiality and expose ambiguities.

Laughter is a close companion of truth. If one ever seriously thinks he has deciphered the truth, then it is a laughing matter. Sri Ramakrishna Paramhamsa would repeatedly tell his disciples that gods chuckle at the seriousness with which we take ourselves. Things seem ridiculous from the heights of Mount Kailash and that is why Sri Ramakrishna asks us to see ourselves through the eyes of god without forsaking our humanness. For him laughter was a grand mirthful expression of our earthly existence – the human-in-divine/the divine-in-human, freedom in bondage and transcendence in immanence. An emotion so deep and so synonymous with truth is so vociferously anti-philosophical in spirit and that is why even Nietzsche's Zarathustra aptly declares, "We should call every truth false which is not accompanied by at least one laugh." If the laughter of Shiva is a sign of humanness, the laughter of humans is an expression of godliness. In this grand dance all boundaries are erased. Everything is ambiguous. The laughing and the laughable God forever exposing a paradox can ease the process of cognising. He uses every persuasive tactic to tutor his subjects. Laughter makes hard truth digestible and for that he is willing to embarrass himself. Laughter is god's remedy to the tedious drone of intellection and Shiva himself with his uproarious laughter shows the way.

Like the heights of Mount Kailash every trait in Shiva is immeasurable, always stretched beyond limits. Terror reaches its peak when Shiva dances in the cremation grounds along with his consort Kali. Adorned with a garland of skulls and sticking out blood-drenched tongue, they dance wildly howling with necrophilic laughter. And yet, their terrifying appearance is an indispensable moment of birth. Their monstrous and ominous dance is the transitional state in which death is sown as seeds for the generative growth of collective life. The *Rudra Tandava* – the angry dance while depicting death in all its horror is not life negating but a pregnant moment about to give birth to a new life. The great devotee of Kali – Sri Ramakrishna Paramhamsa – repeatedly reminds us that Kali's grotesque image is that of a benevolent mother and her wild dance is her regenerative power. Nothing about Shiva and Parvati – the divine parents is, as they seem to be; but they have inner and deeper meanings. The inexhaustible layers of meaning make their character most intriguing and most attractive.

Although Shiva's benevolent nature earned him the title *Vishwabandhu* – 'friend of the universe', he is not without his share of enemies, and the most immediate one is his father-in-law Daksha, whose contempt is without any limit. Daksha refers to his son-in-law as the 'shameless frequenter of cremation grounds' who is always surrounded by 'spirits and ghosts' and wears 'indecent clothes' and 'matted hair' and has uncouth mannerisms and thus berates him as inauspicious. Even Shiva's attendants are not spared, for they are dismissed as 'confirmed heretics' who drink wine, smear ashes and wear bones as ornaments (*Shiva Purana* – Rudra Samhita, Section II). Even in his anger Daksha cannot help but notice the virtues as he ponders over Shiva's paradoxical nature, "Does he come under anyone's control? What is his Gotra (lineage)? What is his nature? What is his job of sustenance? What is his conduct of life? He eats poison. His vehicle is a bull. Mostly he is not a male because of his semi-feminine body. He is not a female as well, because of the moustache on his face. He is not at all a eunuch because his phallus is adored" (*Skanda Purana* IV.II.87.28-35).

Even in his rebuke Daksha is right about many things. Shiva has no father or mother. Unlike his counterpart Vishnu who has taken several incarnations and thus has many parent-figures, Shiva remains omnipotent, for he is the universal father. Hidden in Daksha's bafflement at Shiva's androgynous appearance is one of the most profound aspects of his nature. His *Ardhanarisvara* – 'half-male and half-female' form symbolizes the process of creation by copulation. It is the union of *Purusa* (cosmic soul) and *Prakriti* (cosmic nature) that produces different units of the universe. As one of my favourite images, the male and female, spirit and matter blend in him harmoniously. They are on equal footing; nothing is organised hierarchically.

This certainly appeals to my feminist mindset and emancipated spirit. Once when Shiva's attendant Nandi wanted to prostrate only to Shiva and ignore his consort Uma, the universal parents merged and appeared in one unit as *Ardhanarisvara* to teach him a lesson that mother and father cannot be ranked. They are both equally important. Thus Nandi's chauvinism was subdued.

It is always endearing to watch powerful people show humility and what can be more powerful than a parent's role? Here is one of my favourite episodes in Shiva's tales. Once Shiva was engaged in discussion about the meaning of *Pranava*—the primeval word with his precocious son Skanda and when the son offered to give him a better exposition, Shiva humbly knelt before his son to receive the lesson. This is a perfect Nietzschean equation; the creator does not want blind obedience, rather he seeks a genuine dialogue and takes pride in his creation. The father does not assert his parental authority, instead is willing to recognise his creation on its own terms and bow to its power and intellect.

With his other son Ganesa he does inadvertently exercise his power but eventually rectifies it. Once Parvati was taking her bath and Shiva walked in after overruling his attendant Nandi much to the displeasure, of his wife. Thus the goddess decides to create her own personal attendant and out of the turmeric smeared on her body creates a child and instructs him to guard her private chambers with a clear instruction that no one shall enter without her permission. When the young boy obstructs Shiva's entry he is enraged and a battle ensues in which the boy is decapitated. Unlike the western myth in which the son Oedipus inadvertently kills the father to possess the mother, in this tale it is the all-powerful father that kills the son. Upon learning the truth, Shiva resuscitates his son by fixing the body with the head of an elephant and accords him the status of a Chief-attendant. The father impressed with his son's talent sanctions him with power and manhood. Thus Ganesa becomes the 'remover of obstacles' and, as per the proclamation of all gods, he is to be worshipped before any other god is invoked.

The Supreme Brahman, which is the Primal Energy in essence is One, but manifests itself in many forms as Shiva, Shakti, Krishna, Ganesha and so on, so that individuals can find their own ways of approaching the divine. Each manifestation with its complex personality traits and scriptural episodes has a different appeal. Individuals, based on their specific experiences, have their own truth, and therefore gravitate towards specific manifestation. The Supreme Brahman generously offers a menu of choices for individuals to select their own personal god, responding to specific earthly needs. One can relate to Krishna in so many forms; you could fondle him as your infant, partake in his mischievous acts, play with him as a teenager, have a romantic attraction as a young adult, or he can be your friend and finally your saviour. In short Krishna plays many roles, but Shiva is definitely the father, and it is that role that I desperately seek. For folks like me whose earthly father has been snatched away prematurely, the divine father is the only recourse. For all my life problems I have pleaded with him for help, demanded that he play his role — always seeking compensation for thrusting too many responsibilities on my young shoulders. Like a slighted needy child, I stood at his doorstep constantly seeking attention. Perhaps I took my *Avva's* advice too literally, -"when in trouble go complain to the universal father, people on earth may spit on your face." But wise grandmothers are always right. I always counsel my students, that if they can't find someone who would lend their sympathetic ears to their sob stories, to take a plain sheet of paper and write and in the course of which they are likely to find an alternate plot. To me, more effective than the silent neutral paper or for that matter even a conventional therapist is the conversation with Shiva. I find him to be the most sympathetic therapist. At least I have a frame of reference and can draw various anecdotes from his tales to make a strong case for my grievances. Besides I can freely partake in this wonderfully healing psychodrama, and being an actor, he can respond to it immediately. I can throw a tantrum like a child, I can argue, beg, plead, reason, demand, and surrender. Whatever I do is fine. Being the divine father it is his duty to safeguard his children particularly, the fatherless ones.

Many a tear has been shed at his doorstep, sometimes literally at a nearby temple and innumerable times in my imaginary shrine, always seeking his intervention. Over the years the nature of my demands has been shifting. Clearly he has intervened. In the last couple of years, my persistent request has been to clear the path for Kailash pilgrimage. This request became an obsession and on a human plane it would amount to even pestering an official to consider my application. But then I am this incurable needy child. My mother knows this all too well. She joined me in my flights of fantasy and plunged with me in moments of despair, made her own private appeals, joined me in researching about various aspects of pilgrimage and comforted me when anxiety took over. As a single mother she is all too familiar with her children's desperate search for the lost father. Now it must be reclaimed on another plane. Thus began my prayers, research and preparation on so many levels with a hope that it would culminate in the ultimate pilgrimage.

I wanted my feet to circle the sacred mountain and arms folded in deep reverence to show gratitude. I wanted to hear the sound emanating in that region for the lord of Kailash is *Nada Brahmam* – sound manifest. I wanted to smell the fresh air in that region and bathe in the crystal clear waters of Manasarovar. I wanted to see with my human eyes the physical manifestation of the mythical *Sumeru Parvat* and wanted my tongue to chant a few hymns in its praise, and my skin to feel the spiritual vibrations. This would be the dance of my soul.

THREE

The Beginnings and the Longings—Excursions in Time and Space

The traveler has to knock at every alien door to come to his own, and one has to
wander through all the outer worlds to reach the innermost shrine at the end.

Gitanjali, Rabindranath Tagore

It all begins with a dream, a daydream, that wonderful mid-afternoon dream, when you sit on the window-sill and witness life unfolding in front of your eyes. Growing up in the hot and humid city of Chennai in South India, it wasn't necessarily some exotic scenic beauty meant for a postcard that I saw from the window-sill. I saw the cowherd milking the cow, women preparing cow dung cakes, naked children running around with leaky noses freely defecating wherever and whenever they pleased. I heard men and women screaming at the top of their voices at the water tap in the street corner, and their language was raunchy and ribald and that was a quick lesson in foul language. I saw stern old men walking hurriedly with an umbrella complaining about a decadent society. There were other seasonal passers-by and visitors – the wedding procession, the funeral procession, temple parades and soothsayers, fortune-tellers, evangelists, begging mendicants, street performers, snake charmers and monkey trainers, adding spice to life. In addition there were the regular fruit sellers, vegetable vendors, ice-cream wallahs, cycle-rickshaw wallahs bringing unexpected guests and by dusk time the flower girls arrived with garlands of colourful fragrant flowers. The dust, the heat, the stench and squalour of open sewers and the pleasant fragrance of jasmine flowers all co-existed. The window-sill was my favourite spot; when my parents scolded me I ran to the window-sill and turned my face away, when I wanted to hum a song, the window-sill was my podium, and when I wanted to daydream, which I did very often, there was the ever-reliable window-sill. Tiptoeing to the window–sill was my call, my escape and my redemption. With the cheeks pressed against the iron rods, I dreamt of a world far and beyond. My favourite teacher in school was Mrs. Saraswati who taught history and geography and her words would often haunt me, "Remember girls, your home is not the world, the world is your home, always widen your horizon." Yes, I wanted to see Mesopotamia, Constantinople, Babylon, Java, Sumatra, Borneo, and the Himalayas, the rain forest in South America and much more. But then how? These adults conveniently planted a dream and I was left alone to torment myself. All I could do was scratch the wall in front of me. All the adults in my life were guilty of this crime of sowing a dream and leaving me stranded. My *Avva* – grandmother was the biggest culprit of all for she could with such ease and with such minute details describe *Vaikunta* – abode of Lord Vishnu and *Kailas* – abode of Lord Shiva, and how Sage Narada would traverse back and forth setting up conflicts between *Devas* – gods and *Asuras* – demons.

I remember asking *Avva*, "Is there a place called *Vaikunta* that we can visit"?

And my *Avva's* voice would instantaneously become dispirited and she would lament, "Have I done any meritorious acts in life to see that lord in the milky cosmic ocean" she would say tapping her forehead with her fingers, and go on, "how many more births must I take to get *Moksha* (liberation)? One must have *Divya Drishti* – 'divine vision' to see all that. At least it would have been so much better to be born as a *Rakshasa* 'demon' and reach god quickly. That is what Ravana did. Although a demon, he was a great devotee to Shiva. He went to *Kailas* lifted the mountain and sang the praises of Shiva's dance. But as much as he loved Shiva he hated Vishnu and died in his hands and attained *Moksha* and merged with the God."

" So there is a place called *Kailas*," I quickly interrupted.

"Yes, yes, our Puranas say so, It is somewhere in the North. Great sages and noble souls have gone there. At least there is the mountain and that lake created by Brahma Deva. Hmm," she would ponder and continue, "Tulsi Das said Rama's tale is the *Manasa Lake* in which we must bathe to cleanse ourselves, then perhaps *Mukti* and *Moksham* may be possibilities." The moment Rama came to her mind her voice would rise with joy and optimism, "God gave us the human life so that we may realise his glory." And then the story would continue and peter out into a song on Rama.

Oh! Yes, I know the magic that the story and the story-teller can create. It is said that it is the powerful tool of the primitive man. A necessity for human existence: religion, philosophy, ethics, gods, humans and history – all in one narrative. You should never interrupt grandma's tale; you must simply go with the flow. You can bring other tales and weave with it, but you must never restrict the flow. Like a river it just flows. They were perfect materials to ponder at the window-sill. And like the story teller I hated it when this activity was interrupted to attend to a household chore.

My reality in school was no different, mostly by choice. My favourite classes were History and Geography—everything or anything to do with time and space caught my attention. In addition, in those days to encourage reading, the schools in Madras had special classes called 'Non Detail', in which we studied short stories, fables and novels, and in this class my attention was unwavering. Performance in this class had no bearing on your academic record, and that's why strict academics would dismiss this class as 'time pass'. My Biology and Chemistry teacher never failed to be critical of my skewed interest, "B.V. Lakshmi if only you paid the *deeetailed* attention that you pay in that *Non Deeetail* class you would do much better in science. Of what use is history and geography? Who will give you a job? We Indians love to live in the past glory. Think of the future. **Future**." Her chiding was not effective because even my father who was a voracious reader paid more attention to what I read in the *Non Detail* class and would ask questions on which characters I had met so far and what I thought of them. My father loved books so much that sometimes it was at our expense.

He was more attentive to the printed matter than to the children around him, or the book had to mediate a conversation between him and others. His repertoire was much wider. He loved contemporary history, world politics, literature and spirituality. Some of his favourites from which he would often quote were James Boswell's *Biography of Samuel Johnson*, *Autobiography of a Yogi* by Paramahamsa Yogananda, *A Search in Secret India* by Paul Brunton, in addition Dickens, Hardy and Dostoevsky. Even though my mother equally loved reading books, she would sometimes be frustrated with my father's obsession and occasionally tease him, "if some one asked how many children you had you would probably pause for a moment, but a line from Boswell or Brunton, no problem." With this kind of climate in the household I was destined to be in the window-sill and dream of excursions in time and space. The tale and the globe were too exciting for me to forsake them.

When asked to write a routine essay in school on "what do you want to be when you grow up", almost the whole class said they either wanted to be doctors or engineers and build the nation. We had just read Homer in our history class and I wrote that I wanted to wander off into distant lands like Odysseus, meet new people and experience new adventures. While the rest of the class wanted to *save* the world, I wanted to *see* the world. My English teacher, Mrs. Lawrence was impressed, but my Telugu teacher, Mrs. Subbamma said with some affectionate antagonism, "The whole town goes in one direction, but the little squirrel takes another route." I thought but didn't say, "what the insignificant squirrel sees the whole town misses." Thus the seeds of wanderlust were sown.

As is often the case, when these seeds were sown, I was hardly aware of it. Besides any sign of awareness had to be contained or shoved into my unconscious reservoir. There were too many people asking you to be realistic, set concrete achievable goals and get practical and be in tune with the normative rhythms of life. But being out of sync with the social timetable has become a habit for me and my favourite spot has been that 'dream space' where I can have frequent encounters with gods, mythical figures, literary characters, spiritual masters, heroes and heroines of the past, religious gurus and dead souls. They seem to be my best companions for a good dialogue. When I try to excavate my past and go into the mysterious realm of deep sub-conscious, I recognise some remnants that have conjured up reveries of roaming to far away places. I realise that those suspicious glances from others, particularly someone looking askance at your fantasies, fragments of grandma's tales, melodic tunes emanating from All India Radio, memory-laden fragrance of incense sticks floating in the sacred spots of my household, *prasad* offered at the temple, a book that accidentally fell on my lap, passages read by my erudite father from his easy-chair, all put together could have produced that strong impulse that set the course of my life's journey.

In my early years, it was only the mind that travelled in space and time; my body stayed put. It was too much of a luxury. When pestered about visiting relatives in distant places during summer holidays, my father simply said, "Read Dickens' *A Tale of Two Cities* and you will know all about the French Revolution and read Dostoevsky and you will take a trip to Russia." Instead of a train ticket that I pleaded for, I got a membership card to the local library. Once again the book was my carriage and the window-sill my seat, carrying me to far away places of different time periods.

I was more than eager to liberate myself from the window-sill and be at the historical cross-roads and have chance encounters on major roads, sneak into the by-lanes, scale the uphill road and slide the down-hill road, be at the major intersections to find my denouement of life tale. I no longer wanted to be a spectator of a moving parade, but wanted to be a part of it. The excitement that I sought on the crossroads was quite different from what I got. The adult life on this high road of life began with a tragic accident. Late one night, without any notice, when everything seemed quiet, calm and ordinary, my father died of a massive heart attack. I was 20 at that time and overnight every road seemed to be bleak. Every step on the road felt like treading on eggshells. Thrown into the crossroads, I could neither go back to the comfort of the window-sill nor walk boldly on the road. There were no cheering spectators; only endless, forceful and mocking suggestions on which road I must take. Once your father leaves the earth, everybody with or without much insight takes license to direct your movement on the crossroads of life. It was at this juncture that the tales of the past congealed in my memory storehouse underwent liquefaction. They were no longer antiquated history or imaginary fiction, but living legends to guide my steps. Once my human father departed from the world to go to heaven, I needed the divine father in heaven to descend to earth to take care of my needs. Lord Shiva no longer was an idol in the temple, but a personal god in my heart.

The demise of my father was followed by immigration, confusion, extreme privation, adversities, humiliations and uncertainties. Amidst the chaos, there have been few pleasant encounters. A book that you read, a thinker that you come across does change your life. I say this to my students all the time. It was during my graduate study that I chanced upon the great Russian literary critic and thinker, Mikhail Bakhtin, and he set my feet and my mind in motion. International academic conferences held in his honour took me to various parts of the world, where I could meet the ghosts of my other intellectual heroes. One of the most memorable one was his homeland Russia, a place that gave birth to some of my favourite writers – Pushkin, Gogol, Mandelstam and the highlight of that trip was walking on the famous historical Nevsky Prospect and visiting Dostoevsky's last apartment in St. Petersburg. I had to be a part of Dostoevsky vertigo. Another memorable jaunt was wandering in the 'vales and hills' of the Lake District in England to be greeted by the 'dancing daffodils' so beautifully immortalised by William Wordsworth. For me, visiting any spot saturated with history, whether it be the monasteries in Eastern Europe or the Roman ruins and the glory of Christendom in Italy, or the unpleasant and horrifying events of the past like the Berlin Wall or concentration camps, has been one of the most meaningful events in the journey of my consciousness. Any space without the temporal element is of little interest and when I am in the temporally charged location my mind is hardly attentive to the immediate reality, but travels way back into another time period. In an ancient sacred shrine like *Chidambaram* in India, my mind fails to register the unkempt state of the temple, the wandering beggars, menacing vendors or the corrupt priests, although they are all real, but I am mesmerised by the fact that this was the 'hall of consciousness' where the 'Lord of Dance' displayed his most elegant and robust steps. It is also the shrine that inspired so many great poets and as I walk the temple corridors, their verses echo in my ears. Herein lies the thrill of visiting historical places.

Nietzsche explains the significance of history in our consciousness that sets us apart from other species. He asks us to consider the cattle grazing in a field, they do not know the difference between yesterday, today and tomorrow, they just 'eat, rest, digest' and leap again day in and day out. Whereas for the humans it is that simple phrase 'it was' that tells us what our 'existence fundamentally is' – the very source of our suffering and joy *(Untimely Meditations)*. That's why once a spot charged with history penetrates our consciousness, a rock is no longer just a rock, dust is no longer just dust; they undergo radical transformation and assume a different status in our mind.

If visiting recent historical places is exciting to me, I couldn't imagine what it would be like to visit the timeless shrine of nature. For more than a year before I made the Kailash pilgrimage, I was no longer the desiring subject but was completely besieged by that obsession. I have read and heard that true pilgrimage uplifts the traveller from the prosaic of everyday life into a realm beyond ego, and upon returning one feels truly blessed to make life itself into one single endless pilgrimage. In our daily existence in the dust-filled valleys and low plains, it is difficult to even envision a spiritual galaxy of majestic mountains, calm lakes, flowing rivers, vast expanse of space, cloudless sky and star-lit dark sky capable of purifying the soul. Since time immemorial great sages and saints and other spiritual aspirants have wandered off into the Himalayas for spiritual upliftment. While the majestic mountain range crowning the Indian sub-continent has served as a barrier for invaders and conquerors, it places no hurdles to rid the soul of its impurities. It is one giant purifying machine capable of cleansing the outer ecology and the inner environs.

What is it about nature in its elemental form that allows one to go inward and achieve unity with the Infinite? One of the significant texts of Kashmir Saivism on Yoga, *Vijnanabhairava* – 'Divine Consciousness' offers the most succinct explanation. It says that in open space or in calm darkness where there is no distraction, the individual self has the potential to merge with the Universal Self — referred to as the 'Bhairava' in this school of thought. The text says,

Akasam vimalam pasyan krtva drstim nirantaram/
Stabdhatma tatksanad devi bhairavam vapur apnuyat// 84*

If one, making himself thoroughly immobile, beholds the pure (cloudless) sky with fixed eyes, at that very moment, O goddess he will acquire the nature of Bhairava.

The text recommends that we engage in creative contemplation while gazing into the vastness of sky, because in this process one is bound to be lost in a sense of infinity. When the space inside the head merges with the vast sky, then the seemingly limited space within will become a symbol of Infinity and one begins to feel

---

* Vijnanabhairava or *Divine Consciousness.*Translation: Jaideva Singh that the entire universe is lit by the light of divine consciousness. Similarly, the text recommends meditation in pitch darkness, with eyes closed, so that the light of Bhairava slowly enters the consciousness. There is no better place than the Himalayas to be awe-struck by nature's grandeur. Everything about the Tibetan sky is magical. I wanted to walk on the roof of the world to experience a sense of limitless freedom, and in the words of its beloved saint, Milarepa, I was eager to 'drink the mountain stream'. Where else can one find smoothly curved hills and serrated mountain peaks selectively reflecting crystalline light to produce lucent colours on the landscape? I wanted to be in this sky-dome, where the blue tarpaulin curves over the land, enticing you to touch it. And like many of my predecessors, the mystical longing for the Himalayas firmly lodged itself in the innermost sanctum of my being.

Only a few have actualised this mystical longing. In his autobiography Tenzing Norgay, despite having reached the summit of Mount Everest wrote about gazing in the direction of Mount Kailas from Almora district near the Indo-Tibetan border with awe and wonderment and a deep sense of unfulfilled desire:

> "Sometimes we could look across the border of Tibet and see Mount Kailas, which though only 22,000 feet high, is the most holy of all the peaks in the Himalayas, both to Buddhists and Hindus. Near it are the great Manasarovar Lakes, which are also sacred, and a famous monastery; and through all history pilgrims have come to them from far places of Asia, I wish I too have had a chance to actually go there. But Almora is the closest I have ever been".*

---

* See Tenzing Norkey (1955) *Man of Everest: Autobiography of Tenzing.* G.G. Harrap.

From Almora in India it is only 240 miles to Mount Kailas in Tibet. It seemed so close and yet so far away even for this celebrated Sherpa. Lama Anagarika Govinda so aptly said that to understand the significance of Mount Kailas one has to see it not only "geographically, culturally, or historically, but first and foremost through the eyes of a pilgrim" (*The Way of the White Clouds*, p.305). It was not the mountaineer Norgay who has expressed disappointment, but the pilgrim Norgay for his inability to have reached this nature's shrine.

In a similar tone Pandit Jawaharlal Nehru lamented about the vain expectation of making this pilgrimage in his autobiography:

> " I made many a plan and worked out many a tour, and one, the very thought of which filled me with delight, was a visit to Manasarovar, the wonder lake of Tibet, and snow-covered Kailas nearby. That was eighteen years ago, and I am still as far as ever from Kailas and Manasarovar" (p.38).

Pandit Nehru wrote his autobiography during one of his imprisonments by the British government, and he stated that his dreams about higher valleys and mountains kept him alive during this tumultuous period as he reflected with a mixture of hope and despair:

> "Instead of going up mountains or crossing the seas, I have to satisfy my wanderlust by coming to prison. But still I plan, for that is a joy that no one can deny even in prison, besides what else can one do in prison? And I dream of the day when I shall wander about the Himalayas and cross them to reach that lake and

mountain of my desire. But meanwhile the sands of life run on and youth passes into middle age and that will give place to something worse, and sometimes I think that I may grow too old to reach Kailas and Manasarovar. But the journey is always worth the making though the end may not be in sight"*

In writing the foreword to Swami Pranavananda's classic work *Kailas-Manasarovar*, Pandit Nehru said that he finally reconciled himself to his unfulfilled dream as the narrative and the photographs taken by the author had soothed his longing. In his later years, this personal disappointment was intertwined with political miscalculations and a deep sense of regret and guilt over failing the Tibetan people. Pandit Nehru never recovered from feelings of betrayal when the Chinese reneged on the Indo-China friendship that led to a catastrophic war. This event practically brought about his demise, and the Kailas and Manasarovar region fell into the hands of the Chinese government.

So many people in the past, well-known and unknown had yearned to pay homage to this wonder lake and sacred mountain. Many did not succeed, and only a few got the *Darshan*. Even among those who went all the way, only a select few managed to complete at least one circuit of the mountain. As I started making preparations for this once-in-a-lifetime pilgrimage, with a full knowledge of all the possible impediments along the way, my enthusiasm and anxiety started rising steadily and uniformly. I wondered which camp I would fall into.

To begin with, physically I started on a strict exercise

---

* See, Jawaharlal Nehru: *An Autobiography*. With Musings on Recent Events in India (1936).

regimen, accompanied by consultations with my physician on altitude sickness and other potential health hazards and underwent medical tests, all in an attempt to prepare my body for the journey. Professionally, I suspended much of my writing and made no plans for any academic conferences. Almost everything I read for more than at least 8 months prior to my trip was about Himalayas, Mount Kailash and Lord Shiva. The obsession took over. Nothing else seemed to be important or relevant. Every activity in some form or other seemed to be connected to this spiritual adventure. Never before in my life have I managed to keep myself undistracted, and this is a rarity for me. My wandering mind has consistently been most disobedient and has always refused to stay in one place. The Tamil idiom *Manam Oru Korungu* – 'Mind is a monkey" is the most accurate description of my condition; it likes to flit from one branch of thought to another. This state of mind under certain circumstances can be playful, but when you need to concentrate on a major task like this it is indeed a liability and I had no remedy in my possession. Clearly some higher force kept my concentration steady. Even I was surprised at the discipline that I brought into what I ate, read and thought. However my unabashed craze gave free rein to my fantasies. I knew no bounds, and in the most irrepressible manner my mind started sporting with images and ideas. I wanted to be that freely roaming cloud of *Kalidasa's* imagination, and receive the instructions that he gave to his *Meghaduta* – cloud messenger:

> "Drinking the water of Manasa Lake, the producer of golden lotuses, giving for a moment to *Airavata* (elephant) the gratification of having a covering for

his face (when drinking water), and agitating with
your breeze the sprouts of wish–granting trees, as
though they were garments: - with sportings, full of
various actions like these, O Cloud, you should enjoy
the lord of mountains according to your desire.

*Purva Megha, 65**

Yes, I wanted to enjoy playing with the lord of
mountains to my heart's content. It would be my private
pact with my creator. There are too many unsettled
matters to come to terms with. What better place can
there be other than the adjudicator's primary residence,
which even has a spectacular lake view? In such a serene
location even the divine parents must be in a generous
mood. In his classic text, *Kumarasambhava*, Kalidasa says
that this lake shore is the favourite spot of Shiva and
Parvati for their amorous play. I could perhaps catch
them in good spirit in order to settle my life scores.

---

* The Meghaduta of Kalidasa. Translation: M.R. Kale.

FOUR

Tremblings Along the Journey

There is a reason for this downward journey:
For it is willed where the archangel Michael
Took revenge for that arrogant violation.

Dante, The Divine Comedy

A pilgrim's path is never easy. For that matter it was
never meant to be easy. It is an obstacle race—physically
and spiritually. It is along this rigorous path one may
be able to separate base metal from gold and recognise
deep eternal truths from surface superficiality. In an
obstacle race one cannot circumvent the obstacles; one
must jump, crawl, climb or leap over each hurdle to
reach the finish line. In an arduous pilgrimage the prize
at the finish line is the *Darshan* of divine symbol. Even
if the sacred spot is easily accessible, pilgrims since
ancient times have deliberately and willingly added
hardship in order to reach the innermost depths of their
souls. It is customary for pilgrims before the journey to
make the *Sankalp* – 'ritual affirmation of the intent', and
they may take a variety of vows like abstaining from
certain foods, or walk barefoot or do whole body
prostration around the inner sanctum of the shrine and
so on. These hardships are taken on with a sincere hope

that the rigours of the pilgrimage will ultimately chisel a new improved being.

For any major undertaking to be successful one needs all-round auspiciousness. Many forces must co-operate to make the event a success. It is customary for Hindus at the end of any chanting to invoke the *Shanti Mantra* – the peace mantra thrice as a way of seeking cooperation between the self, the world and the heaven. Disturbances could come from any source. The first *'Shanti'* is invoked to appease the gods, for they must shower their grace and clear the path. All the heavenly bodies – the Sun, the Moon, the Wind, the Clouds, and the Rain must offer their protection and make conditions favourable. The second *Shanti* is for peace on earth, for disturbances could come from fellow beings in the form of individual non co-operation or as social unrest and political turmoil. The third *Shanti* is for peace within the self. In the course of completing a task the mind encounters any number of distractions and disturbances and if the will power is weak one may succumb and not be able to bring his task to fruition. In a spiritual adventurous journey like this some obstacles can be God-sent (*Adhi Daivika*) and they may come in the form of torrential rain, thunder, lightning or heavy winds. That's why one must appeal to each and every one of them for their grace. Secondly, one must be forever conscious of earthly (*Adhi Bhautika*) disturbances, either from nature like floods and landslides or from fellow human beings, and finally the afflictions could be from within (*Adhyatmika*) due to lack of determination, faith or sincerity.

As the departure date approached my mind was preparing for a variety of obstacles and problems, from unfavourable weather conditions to flight delays to personal sickness. I feared landslides, avalanches, thick clouds and fog in the Himalayan region, mechanical breakdown of vehicles along the way, altitude sickness or any other problem arising out of poor preparation on my part. My first tremour came from the most unexpected source.

It was early morning on Saturday, June 2, 2001. I had a good night's sleep and felt a sense of calm, revelling in the goodwill of all my well wishers. My mother gently nudged me and said anxiously, "wake up and read the newspaper, something bad happened in Nepal." My initial response was to brush it aside while my mother turned on to CNN to get the latest updates. I had to jump out of my bed.

Prince Dipendra of the Royal family of Nepal infuriated by his family's disapproval of his fiancée allegedly went on a rampage and sprayed bullets like a madman on his father King Birendra, his mother Queen Aiswarya, his sister Princess Shruti and brother Prince Niranjan alongwith seven other members of the royal family before turning the gun on to himself. Prince Dipendra wanted to marry Devyani Rana of the royal family of Gwalior, India and his family considered the match beneath their status. According to eyewitness account, there was an argument at the dining table and the prince in a drunken rage brought his sub-machine gun and slaughtered everyone around. Some managed to escape and among them was the much-disliked Prince Paras, the son of the present king Gyanendra. This was the worst mass murder of royalty since the Romanovs of Russia, massacred in 1918 during the Russian civil war.

The Nepalese king is seen by his subjects as the living incarnation of Lord Vishnu – the preserver of life, and as such highly revered. King Birendra in particular was much loved and respected by the Nepalese as he represented continuity between past and future. He was responsible for bringing democracy to the country in 1990, and other social reforms that improved peoples' lives. By extension Prince Dipendra was beyond reproach in the eyes of most Nepalese, and therefore the nation was in a state of utter disbelief. They didn't want to believe the survivors' and eyewitnesses' account, that their beloved prince was the culprit. They suspected outside elements or conspiracy. Since all the members of the present king survived, their suspicion was towards them. People wanted to hear that Prince Dipendra was innocent, but the evidence showed otherwise. Frustrated over lack of explanation, people took to the streets demanding the answers that they wanted to hear. In the next few days the mob mentality took over and by June 4, 2001 curfew was declared and security forces were given orders to shoot at sight.

Here in The United States, the State Department had issued travel advisory and cautioned travellers about potential turmoil in the region. Maoist rebels, who have been waging guerilla warfare particularly in the mountainous region, could take advantage of the general instability and attack foreign tourists to draw international attention to their cause. The chaos was at every level and I felt completely besieged by these events. Since the events were so sudden, so gruesome and so unprecedented, no one could predict how they were going to unfold. A day before I was scheduled to leave a few friends of mine called their relatives in

Kathmandu and gave me their telephone numbers as a security measure and gave me some encouraging news. As peoples anger turned into deep sorrow, the curfew was gradually being lifted.

With a sincere hope that the peace loving nature of the Nepalese mind would prevail, and after some earnest prayers I embarked the British Airways flight to India as per schedule on June 8, 2001. The travel agent who picked me up at New Delhi International airport late in the night informed me that the flights to Kathmandu had not resumed, and that there could be possible delays the following morning. He further added that there could be a mad rush at the airport even if the flights resume and I should be prepared for the chaos. Fortunately the flights did resume and I was on my way to Kathmandu.

I got the first glimpse of the mighty Himalayas during the flight, and my earlier anxiety started fading yielding to the rising excitement. Here was the fabled mountain range, so monstrous and proud, defiantly piercing the thick clouds just outside the window of the Indian Airlines Airbus. There was so much dissonance in my sensory inputs; my eyes saw the most spectacular view and my ears heard the annoying sound of the turbo engine, while my nose sniffed the aroma of hot curried vegetable cutlets. In a short flight in The United States all that we get is a tiny pack of peanuts or pretzels. I was surprised at this hospitality. My main concentration was on the perceptual field. The sheer thought that I was going to be amidst the mountains in a day or two, filled my heart with joy. By now my thoughts were travelling at a greater speed than the airbus into that imaginary world of close-up views of the plateaus, mountains, gorges and rivers. I was jolted back to the real world at the very moment the wheels hit the tarmac, and I had to bounce back, resettle and hold the ground.

Inside the airport so many bareheaded men greeted us. I thought that this was perhaps their response summer heat. I purchased the visa on the spot. I repeated several times, 'Sir, re-entry visa'. I couldn't hold the excitement and even added, "I am going to Tibet to see Kailash". With a blank face he pointed to the cash counter and instructed me to pay the fee—sixty dollars for sixty days. I was still intrigued by these shaven heads. My thoughts descended from the heights of the Himalayas to this mundane issue. I was even amused by this nagging thought. Every official there— the baggage handlers, security guards, immigration officials, shopkeepers and just about everybody there had shaven their heads. So many tonsured heads, I have seen only in Tirupathi—a pilgrim town in South India. At the final checkpoint, the official smiled and asked the purpose of my visit. With a broad smile in the unrestrained manner of a New Yorker I said, "to see your wonderful country. I have been dreaming about this place for so long." The official interrupted and said with a sad smile, 'welcome to Nepal' and after a pause added 'the country is sad'.

Only then it dawned on me that this country has been jolted by the recent tragedy. The wounds were still raw and this orthodox Hindu country has been observing the rites of death and bereavement. When a family member dies, Hindu men shave their heads and for the Nepalese, the King is the head of the family. Finally the mystery was solved. A voice within instructed me to contain my excitement. Instead of feeling relief that the curfew was lifted, I was bouncing with joy. It was time to show courtesy and compassion to these hospitable people. As I walked to the gate, I perhaps looked a little lost, but definitely felt a bit embarrassed as my mood was swinging back and forth from personal hope and excitement to cultural chaos and despair. I heard a gentle voice from behind, 'Dr. Lakshmi?' and even before I turned around there was a flower garland around my neck and the gentleman greeted,

'Welcome to Nepal'. Sensing that I looked puzzled the gentleman said, " You don't know me. I am Kinna Sherpa. But I know you. I have a photocopy of your passport."

Kathmandu seemed to be more or less like any other polluted noisy Indian City – very beautiful but with a loud mouth and suffocating bad breath. One cannot help but be vigilant to the traffic coming from all four directions – bicycles, rickshaws, scooters, cars, vans, trucks—honking, deliberately approaching each other, swerving sharply from each other and overtaking each other. I was at loss to detect any method to this madness. Folks here say it is not 'road rage', but a way of life. They don't attach any pathos to this condition. Kinna said in a reassuring tone, "these drivers are very good *Lacchimi Didi*". Once I heard *Didi*, I knew I was in a familiar world. In this part of the world, few minutes after an introduction, an acquaintance is a relative – *Didi* 'sister' or *Bhai* 'brother' or plain aunty and uncle. Feeling a bit reassured my attention was diverted to the beautiful landscape on the horizon and I exclaimed, **"Oh! God, so beautiful, so these are the wonderful mountains?"** Kinna quickly corrected me, "these are not what we call as mountains *Didi*, these are just hills.

Wait till day after tomorrow you will see what real mountains are like."

After twenty years of life in New York City, where only tall buildings and antennas scrape the sky, even a tiny hill seems to be thrilling. I realised how deprived I was of raw nature. On our way to *Hotel Himalaya* Kinna entertained me with his tales of trekking and climbing adventures. He spoke about some of the tallest peaks on earth with such intimacy, affection and reverence as if they were his immediate ancestors with varying personalities. I dutifully played my part as an attentive listener to his ancestral tales. Kinna has even guided an Englishman almost to the summit of Mount Everest. He said that the Englishman got sick just half an hour before reaching the summit and he had to be pulled back to the base camp. Kinna narrowly lost his chance to reach the summit. I felt sorry for his missed opportunity while selfishly feeling assured of being in safe hands, and immediately felt ashamed of my colonial arrogance. Kinna's voice had no such mixture of emotions. When asked if he had any sadness, anger or regret about the Everest expedition, he said with a firm conviction and wisdom characteristic of a Buddhist that a vast array of gods and spirits must shower their blessings for things to go well. Besides, in his view, the good spirits that brought him and his client to safety, were far more overpowering than the evil spirits that prevented them from reaching the summit. I received my first combined lesson on folklore sensibilities of mountain nomads and the wisdom of 'The Buddha Dharma' even before reaching my hotel.

It was time for an orientation that was led by our tour organiser, Mr. Aloke Bagchi – a tall imposing man with a deep voice. He gave us clear instructions on the 'do's and don'ts' during our pilgrimage. He spoke with some grandfatherly affection and sternness of an undisputed patriarch of an extended family. When asked about possible mishaps he was dismissive saying, "nothing will happen, Lord Shiva will protect you." All of us who were proceeding on the journey were to conduct ourselves with utmost decency, care and cooperation. Every now and then he would remind us that we were on a spiritual journey and not on a pleasure trip. For the next 15 days the eleven pilgrims—four Sherpas and the jeep drivers, truck driver and Tibetan guides (who were to join us once we crossed the border) were to live like a family. Mr. Bagchi was a high ranking official at Tourism Department of India and thus seemed to know his business well. He said he has been sending pilgrims to Kailash for the last ten years after his retirement so that he could get his share of the merits of the pilgrimage.

We were introduced to our Sherpas. There was Kinna; our leader who was so calm and collected in sharp contrast to Ming Mar whose nickname was "Kushi" – the jolly good fellow. Mr. Bagchi guaranteed that he was going to make us laugh throughout our journey. Then there was Nimma, who seemed so reliable and trustworthy and finally Zanbo – the cook who promised us delicious meals even in wilderness.

My fellow pilgrims were also an interesting bunch. There was the friendly Prema and since she came by herself I knew she was going to be my partner in this journey. Then there was Advait Bhai and his wife Shree who clearly were spiritual aspirants. Then there was Indrajit Bhai and his wife Kailas and together they exuded quiet strength and strong faith. Then there was Chamraj, who preferred to be called as *Chamanna* and his loquacious wife Jyothi and they were fun to be with. Finally there was a family of three – Suri, Hira and their son Raju who were devout followers of Ganapati Satchindananda Swamy.

The following day we were formally introduced to Kathmandu – the land of gods surrounded by mountains. At the very outset our tour guide said apologetically that we would not visit one of the most important landmarks – the Hanuman Dhoka Palace Complex because of the recent tragedy. Our first spot

Svayambhu Nath Stupa in Kathmandu

was an ancient temple on the outskirts of the city, discovered in first century that has a huge reclining idol supposedly a merger of Shiva and Vishnu immersed in water called *Buda Neelkant*. Despite my familiarity with Hindu temples, the architecture and the temple management struck me. There were no officiating priests or any temple management office. There were only the standard instructions like 'remove sandals' and 'do not take pictures' etc. Legend has it that this idol was discovered, and when an attempt was made to dig, blood poured out of the idol's toe. The idol of full-bodied Vishnu with his conch and discus lying on the *Seshnag* (serpent) indeed looked very antiquated and yet well chiseled and looked quite radiant despite its dilapidated surroundings. Symbolically, this was the chosen spot of *Shiva-Vishnu* for relaxation in cool waters, but in actuality the dirty tank water, the menacing flies and insects and the general unkempt surrounding felt terribly offensive – a regrettable condition of many important shrines.

The Kathmandu valley is the spiritual centre for both Hindus and Buddhists. The great Sakyamuni was born in Lumbini in Nepal and therefore tucked in these valleys are many important Buddhist shrines. According to an ancient legend the Kathmandu valley was once a lake, and on one occasion a beautiful lotus blossomed with divine light atop at the centre of the lake. When Manjusri – the Bodhisattva of learning and active wisdom heard about this, he rushed to the lake and wielded his 'Diamond Sceptre' (a symbol of the indestructible), commonly referred to as the 'thunderbolt' and created a cleft on the southern wall of the hill of the valley to drain the lake in order to reach the divine lotus light. At this holy site a massive stupa was built, said to be around 250 BC.

Located on a lovely hilly rock was that famed Swayambhu Nath Stupa and its architectural design fascinated me. Its main feature strikes one – the spotless white dome symbolising pure Nirvana, and mounted on top of this dome was a thirteen-tiered golden spire, and just beneath the structure there were a pair of 'all seeing eyes of Buddha' painted on all four sides. One is practically arrested in this gaze, regardless of the vantage point. There seemed to be no escape from this gaze and even after departing from this location the eyes seemed to follow me. The eyes were the gateway. One must pass successfully through the scrutiny of these eyes to reach that pure state of Nirvana. Within this massive stupa complex there were several votive shrines and historical monuments and the most notable one was the Deva Dharma monastery, which had a huge bronze icon of the Buddha. The atmosphere in and around this complex was reverberating with the famous Buddhist Mantra *"Om Mani Padme Hum"*. No matter where I walked in this neighbourhood my eyes saw 'THE EYES' and my ears heard the haunting mantra. A shrine is powerful because encoded in its architecture is a symbolic message. It was clear that one must pass the examination of 'THE EYES' to reach the smooth dome of bliss, and the method to reach this goal is to actualise the essence of the mantra *"Om Mani Padme Hum"*.

This Mantra is a gift from Avalokiteswara – the Bodhisattva of compassion and kindness and contained in this brief mantra is the very method for spiritual ascent. *Om* is the primeval sound – symbol for ultimate

Reality, the genesis for all other sounds and all of creation; in it are contained the three modes of nature – conception, maintenance and subversion. The vibration from this sound releases the *Mani* – the lustrous diamond jewel capable of cutting the mind from the bondage of passion and snares of ignorance and illusion. Such a jewel is *Padme* – the lotus flower that grows in the murky lake waters and yet remains untouched by the muddy water even while being nourished by it. The flower is in it and yet not in it and thus an emblem of spiritual development: and *Hum* is the traditional suffix of incantation, representing the trumpeting of an elephant that loudly integrates the preceding sounds and concepts. This mantra is the formula for life; like the lotus flower one cannot completely forsake the entanglements of the earthly life in search of higher goals and shirk responsibility, nor should one be completely submerged in it and allow all the dirt to gather on one's soul.

We visited another equally impressive Boudha Nath Stupa built in the 5th century A.D., considered to be the Mecca of Buddhist pilgrimage, as it signifies atonement of sins. As such, quite appropriately the monasteries in this complex performed intense prayers for the departed souls of the royal family. The friendly monks emphasised that the rituals in particular were conducted with utmost seriousness given the ghastly nature of their death.

Our last pilgrim spot was the famous Hindu shrine – the Pashupati Nath Temple, situated on the banks of River Bagmati, where scores of people were performing the final rites on the banks of the river for the royal family. The presiding deity here is none other than Lord

Shiva as Pashupati Nath – 'the lord of all living beings' including animals. According to the legend, Shiva is said to have sported in this region in the form of a deer and when asked to reveal his true divine form by the demigods he lodged himself here as *Linga* that offers protection to all living beings. Historical records maintain that cowherds discovered this Linga after one of their cows happened to wander away from the herd and showered its milk on this spot. It was upon digging that the herdsman discovered the *Linga*. Since a cow was instrumental in discovering this divine symbol, this sacred shrine got its name Pashupati Nath – 'Lord of cows'. A shrine in some form or other is said to have existed here since 400 A.D. The present structure was built by King Bhupatindra Malla in 1697. All of us offered our prayers and sought the lord's blessings for a successful pilgrimage to his main headquarters – the Kailash.

For all the initial tremors that we experienced fearing political unrest and chaos, the day in Kathmandu was very peaceful, enjoyable and meaningful. I felt a deep sense of gratitude towards the lord of the mountains and continued to petition for a clear *Darshan* of his holy abode. In a single moment my sensations were indeed multiple and heterogeneous. I imagined myself at the foot of the mountain and even in the stillness of that moment, my soul was dancing and crying with sheer joy while my heart was pleading once again for this image to be actualised. Finding no words adequate to capture my mood, I re-invoice the words of the great poet–philosopher of Kashmir Saivism, Utpaladeva from his laudatory hymn *Sivastotravali* – 'Garland of songs to Siva':

"O Lord! Ocean of Nectar!
O Gleaming Three-eyed One!
O Sweet One even of the Monstrous Eyes!"
Let me cry and dance
Exclaiming all this with joy.

With my eyes closed
At the touch of your lotus feet,
May I rejoice,
Reeling with drunkenness
From the wine of your devotion

May I dwell in a glen
Of the mountain of your consciousness
Where lies the uninterrupted state
Of your sublime bliss.

May I live in that sanctuary, O Lord,
Where, taking many forms,
You reside with Devi
From the palace up to the city gates

O Lord may the rays
Of your brilliance beam steadily
Until the lotus of my heart opens
To worship you.

FIVE

In the Himalayan Lap—
Drinking the
Mountain Stream

When I drink at the stream of enlightenment
Or the cool waters of a mountain cascade.
Which is the property of no one else,
Strong tea and beer are both abandoned.
Such easing of the pain of affliction
Is the best way of taking drink –
I've left tea and beer behind.

Milarepa, *Drinking the Mountain Stream.*

The air seemed to be filled with good omens as the day glided in gently over the Himalayan range bringing a cool mountain breeze to which the flowers responded with sprightly dance. The mellowed sunrays selectively pierced the thick early morning fog offering a partial view of everything in sight. I took a stroll in the hotel garden and the place seemed perfectly suited for my morning prayers and meditation. The thick fog suspended in the air and the mental fog that clouds my soul must yield to the bright sunshine. The torpidity within must cede in preparation for the eventful day ahead. The never ending line of smoothly rounded hills and sharply piercing mountain tops, although imbricated rather irregularly, seemed to have their own laws of symmetry, and by every passing moment as the fog dissolved into the sunshine, the mountain faces looked increasingly majestic. My spirit soared as I watched the birds darting upwards to the sky. The early morning dew was steadily evaporating, and the purple flowers on the garden bed discharged sweet scents and everything around and within me seemed buoyant. Mother Nature was in her glory *par excellence* and her sovereign power was benevolently beckoning. Even as my tongue was chanting some hymns in her praise, slowly, without any effort on my part, a verse from *Bhagavad Gita* crept into my mind, as if like a premonition for events to come – "*Sitosna Sukha Dukhesu, Samah Sanga Vivarjitah*". A metaphor for transcendence, the verse asks us to show equanimity in cold and heat and in comfort and discomfort. For the moment the association was very pleasant, but it was clear that this verse was a harbinger for the rugged journey ahead. Like a child securely attached to its caretaker is capable of boldly venturing out in the world, I felt safe and contented in nature's care and having established a pact I was more than eager to tread on the roof of the world.

It was departure time; all the essentials have been loaded in the mini-coach—tents, cooking gas cylinders, stoves, food supplies, sleeping bags, and our duffel bags and other carry on items. Our tour organiser Mr. Bagchi bid farewell to the group and presented each one of us a *Rudraksha Mala* – a protective talisman signifying none other than Shiva himself. The bus set out with a loud chorus '*Har! Har! Mahadev!*

Since time immemorial *Rudraksha* beads have been regarded as very powerful for fortifying the mind and instilling deep tranquility necessary for meditation. In ancient India volumes of Vedic literature were studied and memorised as the emphasis was on both the sonic and semantic element, and students wore *Rudraksha* to enhance intellectual acuity. *Rudraksha* literally means 'Shiva's eye': *Rudra* is another name for Shiva and *aksha* means 'eye'. It is recorded in *Srimad Devi Bhagavatam* that Shiva himself narrated the legend about these beads to his son Kartikeya:

> " I will dwell briefly on the secret cause of the greatness of the Rudraksha seed. Hear. In days of yore, there was a Daitya [demon] called Tripura who could not be conquered by anybody. Brahma, Vishnu and the other Devas were defeated by him. They then came to Me to kill the Asura [demon]. At their request, I called in my mind the Divine Great weapon, named Aghora, beautiful and terrible and containing the strength of all the Devas, to kill him. It was inconceivable and it was blazing with fire.
>
> For full divine one thousand years I remained awake with eyelids wide open in thinking of Aghora weapon, the destroyer of all obstacles, whereby the killing of Tripurasura might be effected and the troubles of the Devas be removed. Not for a moment my eyelids dropped. Thereby my eyes were affected and drops of water came out of my eyes. From those drops of water coming out of my eyes, the great tree of Rudraksha did spring for the welfare of all" (Cantos XI, section IV).

Thus, born out of Shiva's tears, these beads spill grace. It is said in *Shiva Purana* that one of the directives of Lord Yama (god of death) to his attendants is that anybody with *Rudraksha* is to be given its due honour and sent directly to heaven. In one of their conversations Lord Shiva himself declared to his consort Parvati, "the Rudraksha as well as the person who wears it is my favourite" (*Shiva Purana*, Vidyeswara Samhita, Chapter 25). As for me these beads signifying Shiva's tears were meant to wipe out my tears and indeed I rejoiced in wearing them.

The entry into the heart of the Himalayan terrain had a thrill of strange delight as I quivered in its breeze. I was like a little kid taking her first train ride across uncharted territory; my neck craned to the window all the time to catch the scenery from every possible angle. In the early phases the scenery was beautiful, serene and inviting. We passed by several terraced rice fields, flowing rivers, calm lakes and small hamlets. Every frame in this journey would be a delight to a photographer, a painter, a poet or just any wanderer. The resident of a small lonely cabin on the hilltop could be anybody's envy. The landscape changed every minute giving dizzying vistas across the borderland between Nepal and Tibet. At one moment the panoramic view is welcoming and embracing and the very next moment the close up view is prohibiting and challenging. For some time the mountain range is a gracious host; it sprays water from its cascade as a welcoming gesture and gives a leisurely tour of its mansion. Almost instantaneously its nature gets transformed; it begins to snub you with its roaring assertion that it remains unparalleled on this earth. From a distance the mountains seem playful, and as one gets closer they turn monstrous. My neck no longer was craned, my whole body simply cringed and I tightly

The Scenic Himalayan Terrain

held on to my seat. I trembled at the sight of the invisible heights of the peaks, and equally invisible depths of its numerous gorges, dangerous precipices, and roaring water falls and in these conditions genuflection is the only appropriate response.

Our steadily climbing road gradually became an uneven mud-track that had continually been eroded by flowing stream. The path very often was so narrow that driving was indeed hazardous. In many spots the wheels were barely on the ground and the chassis jutting over a deep valley. In case the vehicle stalled at any of these precarious locations, there was simply no way to get out. There weren't even a few inches of ground to set foot on. From the window it felt like we were suspended in mid-air with no safety net. Between the deep valley on one side and the unyielding monstrous boulder on the other side, both ready to devour you there weren't any choices but to wait for providence to show grace. In an ascending path unless the driver accelerates, the coach will not move and with a slight excess in the acceleration the bus could plunge into an invisible valley. There were other dangers as well; landslides at unexpected moments and for us the immediate risk came from remnants of earlier landslides blocking our way. The rocks along with the sticky clay would practically glue the wheels to the ground. In short there was imminent danger everywhere.

In the plains the bus rode quietly; we could hardly hear the sound of the engine, and we pilgrims were chirpy and eager with our eyes fixed to the high skies. Here in the mountains, the bus was moaning and groaning as the driver constantly shifted gears and with us there was pin drop silence. Periodically one would hear deep sighs of relief but most of the time even our breath was audible, and our faces covered with sweaty palms drooped and our eyes were downcast.

I know only one way to release myself from the grip of this fear and it comes instinctually. When danger approaches my lips can respond only with *Hanuman Chalisa*. I don't even need to think and decide what I must chant; it is a reflex action. The Hanuman Chalisa is a lyrical hymn in praise of Hanuman, composed by the great Saint Goswami Tulsidas, the author of *Ramcharitmanas*. Hanuman – the monkey god is one of the most beloved characters in the Hindu Pantheon, particularly favourite among the children. The remedy recommended by adults for children's nightmares of ghosts and monsters is to think or chant the name of Hanuman. This was what my grandmother taught me and that is what my mother tells her grandchildren. I haven't outgrown this childhood practice nor do I want to. This is a time-honoured cure for fear and it works as Saint Tulsidas himself has written:

> *Bhuta pisaca nikata nahi avai mahabira jaba nam sunavai*
> *(24)*

Evil spirits do not dare to go near a person on hearing the name of the great warrior (Sri Hanuman) being repeated.

For now Hanuman must shower his grace and enable our driver to accomplish the difficult task of navigating the treacherous terrain. We feel practically suspended in mid-air, and being the son of Wind-god, Hanuman alone can take us to safety. Hanuman embodies sincerity, speedy intellect, and resourcefulness in addition to several other noble attributes and with his help we can be pulled from this frightening abyss as

The Svayambhu Lingam – a self risen
Phallic emblem in a cave in Kodari

Tulsidas has said,

> *Durgama kaja jagata ke jete sugama anugraha tumhare tete* (20)
>
> By your grace even the most difficult of tasks become easy to accomplish.

Around here the driver must have steady hands and calm nerves, more so than a surgeon performing an intricate procedure, for so many lives are dependent on him. Sensing our anxiety, Sherpa Ming Mar said, "Stay calm, it will be like this till we reach Nyalam and once we get on to the Tibetan plateau it will be better." But then Nyalam is one more day away and for the moment Hanuman was the only saviour. When approaching danger, Advait *Bhai* exclaimed, "Lakshmi *Behen* are you calling out for Shankar Bhagwan?" and I responded, "No, right now the ever reliable *Bajrang Bali* (another name for Hanuman), he is an aspect of Shiva anyway."

Lord Shiva and Lord Vishnu complement each other in setting the universe in motion; they are colleagues in the pantheon and are ready to serve each other. When Vishnu incarnated himself in human form as Lord Rama, Shiva wanted to serve him as an exemplary devotee and out of his *Tejas*-radiance, created Hanuman, a lower monkey form so that Rama would readily accept his service and was born to Anjana and Vayu – the Wind God. That's why Hanuman is referred to as *Sankara Suvana* – son of Shiva and *Vayu Putra* – son of wind. Unlike the Sun or the Moon that illumines the earth only at specific times, the wind blows constantly in the form of vital air serving us at all times and being the son of the Wind God, Hanuman is most immediate and most charitable. With his grace we arrived at our destination for the day – Kodari Eco Resort which was about five miles from Nepal – Tibetan border.

Before trekking up to the resort on the mountaintop, we had our lunch at a roadhouse restaurant situated in a deep gorge on the Kathmandu-Lhasa Highway. In this deep ravine mighty waterfalls hurled from invisible heights into invisible depths with so much force and deafening sound that it was difficult to concentrate even on appetising food. Against the force of these immutable mountains and majestic waterfalls everything seemed so powerless. The partnership between the mountain and the river has been so elegantly romanticised and so boldly eroticised in Indian literature that for the first time I was certain that those great writers and poets were also voyeurs of these intimate moments. The river playfully embraces the lofty mountains showing her curvaceous body, forcefully gushes through every available crevice, swallowing huge boulders along the way, and the mountain in turn affirms its vigour and stamina, blocking her path and navigating her flow. Neither yields to the other, and there was nothing obscene about this rough play. It was just raw nature displaying its uncensored character.

It was time to ascend from the depths of the valley to the heights of the mountaintop where several tiny cottages have been built overlooking the Tibetan town across the border. This was our first taste of trekking up the mountain, which seemed to be an appropriate workout plan for the upcoming 'kora' (Tibetan word for circumambulating a sacred place) of Kailash. We took the only visible track up the lofty mountain with a great

The Majestic Himalayan Range at Kodari
near Nepal – Tibet border

deal of eagerness though not at a stretch, unsuccessfully trying to conceal our anxiety. Like the roaming clouds frequently veiling and unveiling the majestic mountains, every passing moment exposed our rising doubts about this expedition even while our response of exhilaration tried to quickly cover it up. It had all the awkwardness and unevenness of a pre-pubescent infatuation towards a superstar. One longs to have a chance encounter with the much-adored celebrity, but when that does become real one is left speechless, although one may cherish that moment for the rest of one's life. When the misty mountain winds freely blew against my face, I was thrown into wild ecstasies from which I thought I would never mature. This journey, this climb has been a solitary walk to me in every sense of the word. For the first time I realised how animated solitude could be. All these days I thought it was only a poetic muse, but today my body and soul felt so alive in this lone wandering.

Along the way we found a dark cave in which there was a *Svayambhu Lingam* – a self-risen phallic emblem of Shiva. Sherpa Ming Mar said that such self-risen Lingas are scattered throughout the region, and the residents of these localities routinely visit these caves to offer their prayers. Some of us gathered enough courage to enter this pitch-dark cave and saw the Lingam adorned perhaps by some local devotees with some metal ornaments and flowers. Much to my surprise my camera was able to catch the image with its built-in flash. It is said in *Shiva Purana* that *Svayambhu Lingam* has special power and significance since the lord deliberately lodged himself in these remote locations for the benefit of local residents and wandering pilgrims. The text proclaims that "The Svayambhu Linga is Nada Linga" – the self-risen phallic emblem is sound manifest (*Shiva Purana*, Vidyesvarasamhita, Chap, 16, 113=114). Therefore these emblems have special hearing powers; sincere prayer uttered even in the most feeble voice reaches His ears.

Once I reached the mountaintop, I was practically spinning out of control trying to get a glimpse of the scenery from every angle as the dusk fell over the mountains with rapidly changing colours. I came to a halt only when greeted by some of my fellow pilgrims who had been bitten by leeches. These nasty bloodsucking parasites can cause a great deal of commotion, and it was an anti-climax for an eventful day. Once darkness fell, it was impossible to stay outdoors as we were swarmed by dragonflies, bees, and other mountain insects. After a light supper everybody was ready to retire.

While everything was dark and silent and seemed like even the gods may still be asleep; I woke up ready to greet glorious dawn. It was an hour that I was determined to experience to its fullest; an hour immortalised by Sri Aurobindo at the beginning of his epic poem *Savitri*. I looked out of my window and it was pitch dark. Everything around and within me seemed impenetrably obscure and in that inscrutable darkness my half-awakened mind instructed my senses to watch out for a new Day, a divine event and a new transforming force that will slip out of Mother Nature's tenebrous womb. My partially awakened consciousness simply stared into 'Nothingness', not knowing what to anticipate. They say it is darkest before dawn; the mountains seemed to be wrapped up in cozy black blankets. Slowly, but steadily as I heard the murmurings of the approaching dawn, it was clear that the mountains snuggled beneath white blankets. These thick wrappings gradually became thin and transparent and everything around me seemed scantily clothed and I eagerly waited for the stole to drop. There is nothing more frustrating than to catch a partial glimpse of something so enchanting and grand; as my rising curiosity stirred my neutral mind and sedated body I leaped out of my bed to witness this mystique of Nature. There can be nothing more spectacular than the sight of the sun slowly rising over the mountains dissolving the thick fog and gently blotting out the early morning dew. This hour has been the musings of great poets, a meditative hour for spiritual aspirants, and an inspiration for an artist's canvas, a photographer's delight—a sheer beauty for anybody. The melodic structures of Indian music called *Raagas* have captured this mood, and in the midst of my stroll I sat on a rock and started humming some early morning *Raagas* – a few delightful compositions in *Raag Bhowli and Saurashtra* to awaken the gods. Being practically amidst the moving clouds, feeling very alert and awake and sensing everything around me as a blessing, I was in my mind at heaven's doorstep. My imaginative power could not and cannot still visualise a better scene. To heighten this mood further, a very deep chanting of *Om Namah Sivaya* tapped on my eardrums. It was Advait Bhai in his early morning meditation. The mantra was reverberating throughout the atmosphere and when the sound hit the mountain it quickly amplified and sent back with greater force, providing perfect acoustics. Mother Nature showed her benevolence; we sent feeble musical notes and mantras and she acknowledged them with resounding generosity—a perfect feedback to enter into a mystic trance.

A deep prolonged chanting of the sacred syllable *OM* is sufficient to fill the air with mystical vibrations and adding the five syllable mantra *NaMaSiVaYa* was enough to push someone into a trance. It can practically pluck you out of the ephemeral and toss you into an exalted world. The great 16th century Telugu poet Dhurjati, an ardent devotee of Shiva described the power of this mantra as *"Sura Vithi Likhitaksharambulu"* – 'syllables inscribed on the sky' and they are forever alive with movement like the ocean waves. These floating syllables, precious and beckoning direct the movement of the lost traveller like the flickering lone lamp in a dark village. There can be nothing more soothing to the lost soul than these sounds.

Om is the primeval sound called *Pranava* and it is explained by Sage Suta in *Siva Purana* that this syllable signifies an excellent boat to cross the ocean of worldly existence. The significance is in its etymology - *Pra* is a derivative of *Prakriti* meaning nature or the world and *Nava* means an excellent boat and put together it may mean "that which leads to salvation" or "that which leads to new knowledge." The five syllabled word represents the five elements – ether, air, fire, water and earth in perfect harmony. Thus put together, the mantra gives fresh knowledge of both the subtle and gross nature of existence. It is stated in *Shiva Purana* that *Om* is *Dhvani Linga,* which roughly translates into a phallic symbol representing 'sound', echo, noise, voice, tone or tune'. When the tone of this mantra reached the *Svayambhu Linga* – signifying sound in the dark cave nearby, it was transformed into a mystical sound. Advait Bhai's rendition of this mantra with his deep voice and utter concentration ushered in a new day. And we headed towards Tibet.

SIX

BORDERLAND TROUBLES: SEEKING GOD'S INTERVENTION

✟

The transformation of the whole of Tibet into a Zone of Peace.
The first component of Five Point
Peace plan of H.H. The Dalai Lama.

Since times immemorial Tibet has stood as a symbol of humanity's longing for spiritual quest, where there is deep faith in higher destiny of man through inner development and in whose depth the ancient wisdom continues to be an ever-present source of inspiration. As a way of maintaining Tibet as a 'Peaceful Buddhist Nation', His Holiness The Dalai Lama proposed in 1987 that Tibet be declared as a 'Zone of *Ahimsa*' (state of peace and non-violence). Once recognised as such by the global community, Dalai Lama has proposed that the entire Tibetan Plateau be demilitarised and turned into the world's largest natural park or biosphere, where human rights organisation from various parts of the world may set up their offices. Sadly all this remains to be an empty dream, and we witness political atrocities against people who seem to have no political ambition, but simply want the freedom to pursue their spiritual life.

From Nepal we set foot on the Tibetan soil upon crossing "The Friendship Bridge" built over the Bhote Kosi River. We learnt that the bridge was first constructed in 1965 and it was washed away and again rebuilt in 1984. I had a strange feeling of uneasiness not called for as I walked over the bridge. The view from the bridge was spectacular. It seemed as if there was a deep uneven cleft in the mountain range, with huge boulders covered with bushy beards of moss protruding into open space that were about to plummet into the white water several hundred feet below. In addition to the rocks precariously clinging to their parent mountain, there were trees festooned with creepers jutting out from the crevices in every direction. The formation of the dangling tree trunks had their oddities; some grew horizontally, some obliquely turning downwards, and others upwards, some were conventionally vertical, while others were outright upside down. As the mountain winds blew, it seemed as though all the elements of nature have been transformed into trapeze artists. The waving tree branches on the Nepalese side and the swinging branches on the Tibetan side seemed to be in perfect harmony, exchanging lively and friendly gestures. In nature's plan there seemed to be no rancor. How strange, I thought, once political boundaries are drawn, the earth, rocks, leaves, dust and even air take on a different meaning.

Despite the breathtaking view the queasiness within me just wouldn't go away. Just the mere awareness of continued human rights violation in the soil that I am about to set foot on seemed to produce a strong visceral response. I was pleasantly distracted when *Chamanna* said, "Lets us all take a photograph on this Friendship Bridge" and I quipped almost spontaneously, "I sense some unfriendly winds blowing our way and I feel giddy", to which Prema responded rather dismissively, "I think altitude sickness is slowly setting in Lakshmi, you didn't take Dymox tablets". Everybody had a good laugh and after taking some photographs we reached the end of the Friendship Bridge, which is the entry point to Tibet. No, officially it is called China.

The officials at the checkpoint looked like high school boys in uniform, playing tough and looking stern and trying to manage everything by the books. Our Kinna Sherpa spoke to one of these young men and we gathered that our Tibetan Guide team hadn't reached the border to pick us up. Thus it was waiting time for us, sandwiched between two countries, stuck in no man's land; the pavement on the Friendship Bridge was our waiting platform.

For a couple of hours we were the cheering spectators of returning pilgrims from Kailash. I watched batches of pilgrims bid emotional farewell to their Tibetan guides and complete the immigration formalities at the Chinese checkpoint and proceed towards Nepal with a mixture of awe, impatience, envy and reassurance. Our batch eagerly awaiting our onward journey would cheer and greet these blessed pilgrims and bombard them a with a series of questions:

> "Are you coming from Kailash?"
> "How was it?"
> "Did you manage to complete the *Kora*?"
> "Did all the members of your team succeed?"
> "Did anybody get sick?"
> "Did anyone die?"

And the marching pilgrims with a beaming smile, looking very satisfied and contented would say:

"Yes!"
"Spectacular, from every angle"
"Yes, we did the *Kora*"
"Day two the most difficult"
"Go slow on day two"
"Yes people get sick, but it is worth it"
"You will get over the sickness"
"In another group somebody died"
"Don't worry"
"Nothing like that exists on this earth"

These were more or less the standard replies. Yet we continued to ask each batch the same questions, and received similar responses. We could not detain them for a detailed discussion, as they were eager to proceed to Kathmandu. Thus, one thing was clear: the greatest challenge is on 'Day Two' of the three-day circuit around Mount Kailash, and that was couple of days ahead of us. The immediate source of frustration was waiting for our Tibetan guides.

Finally our Tibetan team arrived in 3 Toyota Landcruisers and one truck, and it was time for another adventurous ride to our next destination – Zhangmu, a small town situated on a hill, where the Chinese conduct their official customs clearance. The traffic in the narrow rocky path was rather heavy; trucks, jeeps and porters carrying heavy load form the caravan on both directions. Our Tibetan drivers, although seemed more skillful than their Nepalese counterparts, had a reckless adventurous side to them. Within few minutes into the ride, I realised that our lives were in the hands of these young men for the next 15 days. Every moment seemed like a miraculous escape as we continued our earthly journey in these Landcruisers. Whether one should commend the carmakers for manufacturing such a tough vehicle capable of navigating in the Himalayas, or should we be grateful to the dexterity of Tibetan drivers or is it some divine power that directs the chaotic traffic to safety is an open question. Perhaps all of them combined with our *Karma* played a role.

And so we ascended, bumping and thumping passing through some narrow waterfalls (a free periodic car wash), negotiating tight turns, constantly tossed in every direction. There were no seat belts to secure us tightly. At every hairpin turn, the path was dangerously eroded, and the road rose steeply exactly where the turn was the tightest. The ascending ride from the Friendship Bridge to Zhangmu is no more than 30 to 40 minutes, but it seemed like eternity, after so many close calls.

Finally, we reached the official border town of Zhangmu, where the road at any point is either a climb up or a descent down. The ground beneath my feet was never flat, and the world around me seemed to be spinning out of control. I have never in my life consumed any more than few sips of liquor or any other intoxicating substances; therefore I had no frame of reference to explain my current state of mind. I was undoubtedly feeling tipsy, lightheaded and nauseated – perhaps an acute attack of altitude sickness. Prema chided me for not taking Dymox[1] tablets.

After preliminary clearance by the Chinese officials, the Sherpas took us to a nearby restaurant, while they

---

[1] Sherpas recommend Dymox tablet as preventive measure for altitude sickness.

completed other required formalities. When we got into the restaurant, the weather outside was balmy, breezy and pleasant and slowly I was coming back to my senses as my giddiness started fading. Within a matter of few minutes dark clouds hovered over the sky and we were to get our first experience of Himalayan storm. Just a moment ago Mother Nature seemed to be her benevolent self, and my twirling senses were coming to a slow halt, and the very next moment she seemed to unleash her wrath and the thunderous scene outside once again threw me into a discombobulated state. A little while ago, I was in an inebriated state, neither induced by liquor nor by any spiritual ecstasies; just body's response to relatively thin air, and as I regained my gait and was able to hold ground I was amused at myself and the world around me. Nature does play its tricks; perhaps it had its own version of harmless mirth. Almost instantaneously it shows its other facet, with blinding lightening and terrifying mountain-roar, it was pouring torrential rain accompanied by heavy winds. The sloping road is now transformed into a gushing river. It is a miracle that the parked vehicles were not washed away.

After a grand display of nature's fury, the show came to an abrupt end. The rain stopped, as instantaneously as it started and suddenly everything looked calm and peaceful. The skies looked clear and bright, the Sun was shining and practically within few minutes everything looked dry and clean. It looked as if the celestial bodies just wanted to show their character: *Vayu Dev* (the wind god) and *Varuna Dev* (the rain god) displayed their intense nature and were soon overpowered by *Surya Dev* (the Sun god). If only we had a better scenic view, we could have seen the rainbow arch over the mountains. But right now we had to wait for the Chinese officials to give clearance and issue the road permit.

The Sherpas walked into the restaurant rather hurriedly and we thought it was time for us to proceed through our journey to the camping site. There was no such luck. The Chinese officials wanted a detailed search of our baggage, and we grudgingly unloaded our luggage. The search was thorough; our clothes were unfolded, pockets emptied, wrapped materials unwrapped, sleeping bags spread out, snacks and other eatables carefully examined and smelt (we tried to humour them and offered a bite and they refused with a straight face), and finally even the pouch of a sanitary napkin was not spared.

When it came to my baggage, I had something else that seemed to raise their antennas. I had some xeroxed pages from Swami Pranavananda's book 'Exploration in Tibet' and 'Kailas – Manasarovar'. I also had some copies of maps of that region and a sketch of mountain peaks in that route. They were just reference materials in my mind, but clearly they raised so much suspicion. In addition I had Jetsun Milarepa's book 'Drinking the Mountain Stream: Songs of Tibet's Beloved Saint' and Wendy Teasdill's 'Walking to the Mountain: A pilgrimage to Tibet's Holy Mount Kailash' foreword for which was written by H. H. The Dalai Lama.

The young officer, looking like a pre-pubescent boy with smooth skin pulled them out hurriedly with such seriousness that I quickly intervened using both hand gestures and words, " I like to read books when I am travelling ... going to see the mountain and lake", I said a bit apologetically. Even before I could finish my sentence, the young officer clutched my papers and books and disappeared into the corridors. Instinctually, I held my arms close to my bosom feeling terribly violated. I felt as if someone was snatching away my baby. These printed materials are my constant companions, and how dare a young boy, who could as well have been in my classroom, so disrespectfully seize them away. Being possessive of books, and not being used to lending them even to close friends, this act seemed like a dagger piercing deep into my soul.

After a long wait, the young officer returned with another officer, perhaps his supervisor. I lunged forward to collect my papers and offer an explanation and the officer signalled with his hands to stay put. The mystery is getting deeper. After a long pause, the senior officer looked at me and said,

> "You ... Professor?"
> "Yes". *But how did you know?* I thought, and then added an unsolicited response,
> " they are reference .. going to Kailash".

He looked at me with a blank face. Clearly he seems to understand English; after all he was reading my papers and books.

> "Exxxploration in Tibet?" he seemed to query holding my xeroxed pages.
> "Yes". I thought it is better not to offer any more explanations.

He slowly unfolded the map and I said quickly adding some hand gestures,

> "reference .. I like to know where I am".

Once again no response and after a long pause he held one of my books and said,

"*Drinking the Mountain Sssstream*"
"Yes a book of songs", I said with some indignation.

And then he looked at the other book and said, '*Walking to the Mountain*'?

I nodded.

His attention was now riveted to the top of the book and tracking the words with his index finger he read, "Foreword by the Dalai Lama."

Oh! My God! I knew I was in for some trouble. But what could I say or even gesture. If an index finger can kill and if silence can speak volumes, this was the moment. By now my knees were shaking and I was visibly restless. Once again both the senior and junior officers walked away with my papers and books. For the first time in my life, a book became a liability and I had in my possession all the dreaded words – 'Tibet', 'Tibetan Saints', and 'Dalai Lama'. Am I going to be interrogated? I am not going to be apologetic. Perhaps I should have been a bit more politically astute and left the books behind, instead I brought along my favorite travel companions – reference materials and a book of songs. Legend has it that Milarepa performed many miracles at *Kang Rinpoche*, and we were to visit the cave he meditated in and having some of his words handy would, in my mind be a perfect excursion into the mythical past. What a sentimental fool I was. I should have known the political realities better. This self-loathing was accompanied by a tinge of guilt. Did I place all other pilgrims at some risk? After sometime the officers returned and handed over my books and papers and I looked stunned not knowing what to make out of this situation. The junior officer gestured that I may re-pack my bag.

Once we walked out of the customs office, Kinna told us that we would halt at Zhangmu that night and there were two reasons. One was that there was a huge landslide just half a mile away along our route and it would take a couple of hours to clear that. But more importantly we were not issued the road permit to proceed.

"But didn't you get it earlier?" all of us questioned in a chorus.
"No this is routinely given here", Said Kinna
"Then why not now?" we asked
"No explanations. Please understand that from now on 'PROBLEM' will be our close friend", replied Kinna

I was even more puzzled and said to Kinna, "but you look so calm", to which he replied in a matter of fact manner,

"We have done this so many times, always there is some problem or the other"
"But why" I asked.
"Don't ask too many questions *Lacchimi Didi*, don't worry we will go tomorrow". Kinna assured and added; "besides we have to buy vegetables. The Chinese took all our vegetables and canned foods".

I was getting even more horrified. The Chinese confiscated perishable food supplies worth Rs.10,000 giving no explanation. We gathered that they re-sell the goods in the town and stranded pilgrims have no choice but to purchase them back. The Sherpas narrated these incidents casually, as if it is a routine. Ming Mar joined in and tried to make light of the situation, "this is a blessing...bad landslide...it is dangerous...Buddha is kind...and off we go tomorrow."

A nasty landslide *en route* and Chinese bureaucracy left us stranded in a dingy hotel with no hot water or bathrooms, and the common toilet facility with peculiarly shaped lavatories was just bearable. Despite knowing fully well that baths and showers are not going to be possibilities in this journey, the dirty toilets created a deep sense of disgust. At least we are able to humour ourselves on matters of scatology to make the conditions bearable. Thankfully, we were provided with some hot water in a flask, so sponge bath was an option.

There were other peculiarities as well: the clocks in Tibet are set to Beijing time, and therefore there is a disjunction between clock time, and nature's time. How ironic, I thought, political forces go against natural rhythms of sunrise and sunset. This had an immediate impact on our journey. For reasons unknown our road permit had to be issued in Lhasa, and by the time they open the offices, it is already early evening, by nature's clock in Zhangmu and that meant losing precious time.

Well, we are in Tibet and these inconveniences, uncertainties, injustices and adversities are sending some hidden messages. Earthly life is chaotic, unjust and erratic, and therein lies the need for a wise mind. That's what evolved souls and learned sages from this region have said all along. We have to choose our battles, know how to wage them and decide when to wage them. To find suitable armaments for this combat, one must traverse the inner landscape. Meditation was the only remedy that I could find to calm my disturbed mind.

The following morning Prema joined me in my prayers and together we chanted several hymns. There was no point in worrying over how the day was going to unfold. Rejoice in what every moment can offer. That's what Tibetans do: they seem to know how to extract delight out of even the bleakest situation. Thus we considered it our blessing to have Jeetendra, a migrant worker from India who was the waiter / cook in the restaurant adjacent to our hotel. This pleasant young man managed to prepare dishes to our liking. The rest of the day, we were once again spectators to a parade of returning pilgrims. Many of them said that they were also detained like us for couple of days for unknown reasons.

Every now and then the Sherpas would gather some rumours and gossip from the streets and relay them to us. According to their sources, the U.S. Passport holders, in particular were singled out for this kind of harassment and a vast majority, about 95 percent of them, Ming Mar declared dramatically, were denied permission to proceed. The reason – it was a retaliation against a tragic mid-air tiff between U.S.A. and China earlier that year. In April 2001, there was a mid-air collision between one of United States Navy surveillance aircraft and a Chinese F-8 jet, resulting in the death of the Chinese pilot. China demanded full apology, and U.S. described that as a tragic accident. The Sherpas further added that for sometime Indians were given a cold-shoulder due to some other political tug of war.

If there is any validity to these rumours, then it leaves us in double jeopardy. I couldn't begin to grasp the vicissitudes of this recent political wrangling, and my mind generated series of unanswerable questions and doubts. Can there really be a direct cause and effect relationship between politics and pilgrimage? After all we were not a political team, just a bunch of pilgrims in spiritual pursuit. Can there be a simple explanation for this? A clerical error perhaps, or incompetence on the part of our trekking company or is it our bad luck? When explanations are not given the mind entertains all sorts of idle conjectures. On the other hand our languishment under these unknown, unjustifiable conditions seem to support our suspicion of foul play by Chinese officials.

Our second day of waiting did not yield the necessary road permit. Kinna looked discouraged. He asked us to be patient and wait for another day and that his trekking company would use their influence (the sub-text is that they would bribe) to extract the permit. The following day would be the decisive day; if given the permit we would proceed to Kailash otherwise return to Kathmandu. In his estimate waiting any longer wouldn't be feasible, because the lost days cannot be compensated and driving after nightfall would be virtually impossible and he was not willing to compromise on our safety. Furthermore, the Chinese would never extend our Visa if needed. It was late in the evening and Kinna said to all of us in a despondent tone, "Pray to Shiva, see you tomorrow."

It was the longest night: each time I tossed and turned, my thoughts were racing through so many topics – political atrocities, religious persecution, metaphysical debates, individual *Karma* and none of them yielded any satisfactory explanation. Multiple voices kept ringing into my ears, and one voice from within instructed;

"Pray to God."
"Without Shiva's consent even an ant won't bite."

"Appeal to a higher authority."
"The Lord of the mountains alone can give the clearance."

There is no doubt in my mind about divine power, or on faith, prayer, ritual or worship. But the questions in my agitated mind were entirely on a different plane. The high flown eternal dictums entered into a peculiar dialectic with ground political realities and the two were never going to synthesise. For every grand proclamation from the high-skies, I had a nagging *'but'* response:

Yes, God is great, wonderful, merciful and sagacious. But in what way is he responsible for the petty politics of the Chinese government? For all the human errors, it has become a habit to hold God accountable. It is not God's fault that Dalai Lama had to go into exile. It is not God's fault that thousands of Buddhist monks have been shot dead. Their devotion is certainly not in question.

I became defensive towards god and skeptical towards the Chinese. I remembered the Dalai Lama's account of his land and his people, and their ongoing battle for religious freedom with the Chinese, and I wept along with every wounded, humiliated and tortured Tibetan. All these days knowledge of these atrocities lurked in my mind and it was merely an intellectual exercise on human rights. But today, every blow to the unyielding Tibetan hit me, every act of desecration enraged me, every bonfire made out of their sacred books charred my skin. And so I vowed, like a devoted squirrel[2] in Ramayana, that I would join the peaceful cadets to draw attention to the plight of Tibet. The world has seen what

---

[2] An army of valiant monkeys builds a bridge across the sea for Lord Rama. A little squirrel wants to do its part, and therefore rolls over wet sand at the sea coast and goes to shake off the sand at the construction site.

the Chinese are capable of doing to their dissenters in broad daylight at Tiananmen Square. If they are ruthless enough to ram army tanks on their youngsters under the full glare of cameras from every part of the world, what kind of horrors would they not resort to when they are not under surveillance?

The call for action against Chinese ruthlessness was for a future date. But tonight I still have an immediate problem at hand, causing deep anguish in me. What will happen tomorrow? Once again multiple voices of fate, *Karma* and *Kismet* hurled some unpleasant predictions:

> *"If it is written on your forehead it will happen."*
> *"If you have done some meritorious acts in your previous life you will reap its rewards tomorrow."*
> *"If god wants you at his doorstep he will remove all obstacles."*

Once again I have to confront the demons in me. Am I worthy of this pilgrimage? If rejected I shall add this to my long litany of woes. I seem to have become an expert at adding more items to this list. Each time I tossed and turned, evil forces in the skies seemed to laugh at my predicament, loudly announcing all my failures and disappointments – early loss of father, saddled with family responsibilities, painful separation from my *Avva*, doomed passions, failed relationships, uncle and aunt murdered, professional disappointments, personal inadequacies, derailed from the normal and typical course of life events, undue delays in achieving goals, and all these amidst economic hardship. My life has been colourful enough. I thought the pilgrimage would be the compensation for all other woes. But turned away at this juncture would feel like ultimate rejection. Will God send me back empty-handed?

Would he really send me back empty-handed after instilling such a strong desire? As I faintly murmured these words I broke into tears and wept like a child.

Another rollover in the bed, I now became indignant. I was piqued and God was held accountable:

"You have made it your business to send me empty-handed. What do you expect from me? What kind of abnormal standards do you hold me to? If I erred, tell me how to correct it. Otherwise why bother sending me into this world and leaving me stranded. I thought that is the duty of every parent. Considering that my biological clock has ticked away and I am not going to know what it means to be a parent. I only know one role – the child and right now an angry child throwing temper tantrums. I don't know about meritorious acts of my previous births. You did not equip me with that cognitive faculty. All I am left with is this birth, this life and in this life I want to see Kailash. I thought you were compassion-incarnate, so if I blundered please forgive. Unlike Vishnu-the trickster, you are gullible – the adorable Bhola Shanker and you are not in the business of testing anyone – not even the demons with sinister motives. Why am I being tested? I don't want to know about all other deserving candidates who have been turned back. Wherever you are listen to my desperate cry and respond."

This fury within me, just by sheer fatigue calmed down and I turned repentant.

"Oh! God! Forgive me. Forgive me for having the audacity to dare you. I am so desperate. Please don't put me in such a pathetic state. I am all too familiar with this equation between you and me. I am always asking you for some favour or the other, seeking your attention like a slighted child, pestering you to intervene in some earthy trouble, although they are perfectly acceptable. When in desperation, I have been the recipient of your boundless compassion. There is no doubt

about that. But now I am seeking a dance with you, a bold joyous dance, so that in confidence I can feel your grandeur. Yes, that's what I want. That's what I want. I am sure you are listening. Whatever happens tomorrow I can't blame you. I might be angry at the turn of events, but you are beyond reproach. Whatever happens I have to come to you anyway. We can't forsake each other. This is a guaranteed bond.

And so the cycle of self-loathing, self-affirmation, angry praises to God, desperate pleas to God and justified resentment towards the Chinese government repeated throughout the night.

The decisive day in my life slided in and despite being in the heart of the Himalayas, I did not and could not notice it. I was stuck in this stinking dungeon-like room in a hotel that did not even offer a glimpse of the mountain or the sky. The gloomy surroundings added to my despondency and I had to find some way of infusing life forces. I chanted some hymns and prostrated myself full length on the ground in what I thought was in the direction of Kailash. It was for the love of the mountain, love of its resident and a sincere hope for divine aid that I paid my obeisance. I knew that if I reached the mountain it was only by the power of divine grace.

In my half-melancholic state I walked into Shree and Advait Bhai's room. It was impossible to force a conversation on mundane matters when the stakes are so high. Another emotional outburst and another collective affirmation of the power of the divine parents residing in the mountains followed. Advait Bhai is truly a spiritual aspirant – his love of God is intense, his method of knowing God very rigorous, and his knowledge on spiritual matters, in particular Sri

Aurobindo's writings very sound, and above all he is gifted with a deep melodious voice. There was no point in commiserating on the present state of affairs, and Advait Bhai spontaneously gave us the remedy. He rendered some appropriate hymns musically; an urgent, sincere, devoted 'SOS' calls to the Universal Mother. The realised souls in the past have always asserted that when in distress, God comes in many guises to reassure, and this morning the consolation came from Advait Bhai's voice.

After a brief musical interlude, feeling rejuvenated, we went to our usual meeting place – the restaurant adjacent to the hotel. Slowly one after the other all the other pilgrims arrived. The anxiety was palpable; neither could one engage in mundane conversation, nor could anyone be upbeat, and above all no one wanted to add to the moroseness. The Sherpas joined us and they looked discouraged. Their usual 'don't worry' was replaced by 'let's see'. Kinna asked us to vacate our rooms and assemble in the lobby. By afternoon, in his words, 'if a miracle happens', we proceed, otherwise go back to Kathmandu. Our friendly waiter/cook, Jeetendra, perhaps sensing the seriousness on our faces prepared delicious brunch and played a cassette of '*Shiv Bhajans*' – devotional songs on Shiva. I tried my best to keep my emotions under control, but my moist sockets disobeyed. So many great *Bhakthas* – devotees in the past have composed songs, written the finest lyrics to express their pain when distanced from their Deity, their words came to my mind. As a student of classical music I have learnt many devotional renderings and am familiar with many others, but for the first time in my life I had to put that essence into practice – the only option I have is to surrender. Yes, SURRENDER to the highest authority. Once this dawned on me, my eyes stopped shedding tears in recognition and acceptance of a Higher Force.

Prema and I walked back to our rooms, assembled our bags in one pile and waited silently for the porters to pick them up. They were already schlepping bags from other rooms on the 5th floor, where our group was staying, and we watched everything in disbelief. Suddenly we heard a voice calling our names,

" *Are O! Lakshmi and Prema*", and we saw Advait Bhai running up the stairs, huffing and puffing,

" We have some good news and bad news", he exclaimed, and then continued, "we got the road permit".

" Then what's the bad news?" we asked anxiously.

"The Chinese won't accept a faxed copy of the permit from Lhasa, so the trekking company messenger is driving all the way here. He should be here tomorrow morning, 700kms".

All of us rushed to the lobby and Kinna had a smile on his face. He said, despite the lost days, it is still doable and added, "if the weather does not permit we won't be able to do *Kora.*"

"But if the weather is OK we still have the days right"? I asked. Strange, a moment ago I was willing to settle for a *Darshan* of Kailash and now my expectation was rising.

All of us pledged our cooperation; we said we will get up at 4 AM or even earlier if necessary, cut vegetables, help pitch tents and so on. We were promising more than what we were capable of and Kinna knew that very well and said, "relax today, from tomorrow it will be very hectic."

Our prayers were answered. That afternoon I had time to reflect. All night I battled: I wrestled with ideas, posited arguments and counter-arguments and couldn't get past my academic habits. When that didn't work, I threw up a tantrum, despised myself and again pleaded for my case. I presented my credentials, and like my bargaining students, I too asked for a better grade even if my work was not up to the standard. I took out my frustration on the Divine Parents and blamed them for my woes. I hated myself for this and wept, harping on the sympathy factor. Nothing worked. I finally surrendered and then....

SEVEN

ON THE ROOF OF THE WORLD

Here, traveller, pause and think, and duly think
What happy, holy thoughts may heavenward rise
Whilst thou and thy good steed together drink
Beneath this little portion of the skies.
Wytheburn Chapel and Inn, Hartley Coleridge

The journey today had a dream like quality; everything in and around me seemed to be a gift of life. I asked Dadu, our Tibetan guide to show me that blessed road permit. For a moment, I took its blessedness too literally and examined it closely with my eyes and hands, hoping to find the seal of god's kingdom embossed on it. Life occasionally seems to inflict pain only to accentuate the pleasures to come. Thus, everything today seemed doubly grand and enchanting. Once again, we were going higher and higher, the moving clouds playfully blinding us and then passing on to envelop the virgin forest, the rocks, the mountain peaks and the gorges and the view before us was swiftly changing revealing breathtaking grandeur for one moment and blotting it out the very next moment. The suddenness with which the scenery changed seemed uncannily witty. This was nature's magic show; everything seemed transient, but never frustrating. One picturesque view was quickly replaced by another. Even our uneven path tossing us in our vehicles didn't seem frustrating at all. It was Mother Nature's way of cradling and rocking. At the most unexpected moments we were showered by a rush of water descending from the mountains and our capable drivers managed to lurch through, giving us the thrill of a lifetime. For the first time, I had clouds above, clouds below and clouds besides me, and I was thrown into a hypnotic trance. Our ascent continued and we darted through one cloud-layer after another. What seemed to be the white sky above one moment became the white sea below the next. It was a mystical journey through different world-planes into a region far and beyond. The thinking machine simply shuts down; it just seems too feeble and inadequate to register what the sense organs absorb.

I felt bewildered in the plexus of moving clouds, spraying water, sunbeams and blowing winds. Everything seemed beyond this human existence. Entangled in this cosmic system and stung by it, I was incapable of distinguishing between real and unreal, sentient and insentient. Are the gates of heaven opening? This entry into the world of luminous colours under deep blue sky that seems so touchable, the winds blowing against the robust mountain walls producing sounds unheard before, and the snow-covered slopes lit up by fierce sunshine that is blinding produced such an eerie feeling that I felt I needed some 'divine vision' to tolerate the radiance.

It is one thing to dream of magnificent forms, great heights and glorious nature and another thing to actually be in it. What was exciting in the imaginary

Ascending through one cloud – layer
after another in the mystical Himalayas

world is overwhelming in the real world. Even the
chosen disciple of God, Arjuna shuddered when granted
a vision of the Absolute Form of the Divine. Arjuna,
having heard the highest spiritual secret directly from
God, wanted to see the living image of Spirit and Power
and asks Lord Krishna to reveal his Divine form. The
Lord, knowing fully well that the human eyes cannot
grasp the form that he was about to witness, sanctioned
him the 'divine eyes'. Arjuna having seen the wondrous
form, the luminous mass of energy on all sides, realises
that this form is the object of veneration, at once
delightful and reassuring and dreadful and terrifying.
After seeking forgiveness for his rash vehemence, Arjuna
pleads to the Lord:

> Adrstapurvam hrsito smi drstva
> Bhayena ca pravyathitam mano me
> Tad eve me darsaya deve rupam
> Prasida devesa jagannnivasa

I have seen what never was seen before and I rejoice, but
my mind is troubled with fear. O Godhead, show me that
other (human friendly) form of Thine; turn Thy heart to
grace, O Thou Lord of the gods, O Thou abode of this
universe.

Bhagavad Gita, Chap.11, 45

The vision of anything so exalted and radiant produces
a deep sense of unworthiness of the self and
worthlessness of material pleasures. When Isaiah in the
Bible saw "Lord sitting upon a throne, high and lifted
up", he said with humility, "Woe is me! For I am lost;
for I am a man of unclean lips, and I dwell in the midst
of a people of unclean lips; for my eyes have seen the
King, the Lord of hosts!" (Isaiah 6). As our caravan went
up and still up in the majestic Himalayas, revealing It

is a dusty town situated at an altitude of 12,200 feet, and from here onwards, there is no more greenery. Its famous landmark is the cave where Milarepa, Tibet's beloved saint, born in 1052 meditated and performed miracles. His early years were filled with misfortunes, hard labour, poverty and humiliations and he responded to these hardships with crime and sorcery. Much later he repented for his sinful deeds and sought salvation through the practice of Dharma. He came under the tutelage of an Indian Guru – Marpa, whose methods were rather rigorous. Marpa imposed severe mental and physical penance and finally accepted Milarepa as his disciple and taught him the principles of Dharma. Milarepa is said to have meditated alone in this cave for eleven continuous months and finally attained direct Realisation and was set on the Path to Bodhi. I was so eager to see this cave in Nyalam, but to our misfortune the Chinese bureaucracy had already robbed four precious days from our trip and we couldn't afford to lose any more time. I had to satisfiy myself reading some of his verses. Besides, Milarepa himself was no stranger to adversities and injustices and in his own pilgrimage he had to explain spiritual pursuit to his unsuspecting audience through simple songs. To those who scoffed at him, Milarepa said in his melodious voice:

> I pay homage to Marpa the Translator,
> I who sing the ultimate essence of being,
> Sing the song of [Seven] Adornments.
> You mischievous demons here assembled,
> Lend your ears and listen closely to my song.
> By the side of Sumeru, the central mountain,
> The sky shines blue o'er the Southern Continent;

Gold and Copper coloured hills on the Tibetan Plateau.

The firmament is the beauty of the earth,
The blue of heaven its adornment.

The Journey to Lashi, The Hundred
Thousand songs of Milarepa

Milarepa himself has clearly instructed to meditate on
the Snow Mountain and so we moved on.

The journey in this 'in-between zone' was indeed
mystifying. This region practically shares no features
with the earth below, and having shed all its greenery,
this vast land with curves and folds seemed to be in the
most intimate relationship with its primordial partner
– the open sky. This highland that has risen from the
earth seemed to have been transformed into a majestic
pavilion of arts with the sole intent of putting on a grand
cosmic show. This is the stage where the lord of dance
with his celestial choir dazzles the universe with his
graceful movements. Even before the show begins, one
is astonished by the architectural details of this theatre.
Gold and copper coloured hills seem to stretch into
oblivion only to be contrasted by the snow-covered
peaks in the background, and arching over this
immensity is the 'blue' sky. No artist on earth can
capture the intense luminosity and clarity of that
'blueness'; it would simply pale before this 'blue'
Tibetan sky. The sharp sunbeams illumine every form
and design with exquisite clarity. The mid-afternoon
breeze criss-crossing the mountains had its own
eccentricities; sometimes it was gentle and pleasant, but
most of the time it heaped mountain dust on our bodies.

In this desolate vast land there are no man-made
structures. Occasionally we would pass by some ruins
of dilapidated constructions that perhaps were once a
monastery or some other place of worship. Whatever

these uninhabited buildings were, they have been demolished in a haphazard manner during the Cultural Revolution. The Chinese had their own methods to get Tibetans to shed their ancient beliefs and practices. Clearly, these spots have some historical and mythical significance, because the rock cairns festooned with prayer flags are still intact.

Travelling on the roof of the world where the space and silence overwhelms you, one feels so small and miniscule. The land and the space dominate you. Despite the feeling of diminution of the body, I felt my consciousness stretching and widening out like my outer world and at the same time it would contract and go deeper and still deeper into my sub-consciousness revealing some deep secrets about myself and the world. Ostensibly, as the consciousness was extending and broadening into vacant space, it needed a firm anchoring spot, and could only turn inward. This phenomenon is explained in *Vijnanabhairava* – an ancient text belonging to the school of Kashmir Saivism and it says thus on the connection between consciousness and space:

Nirvrksagiribhittyadidese drstim viniksipet/
Viline manase bhave Vrttiksinah prajayate// 60

One should cast his gaze on a region in which there are no trees, on mountain, on high defensive wall. His mental state being without any support will then dissolve and fluctuations of his mind will cease.

Abhinavagupta, a great commentator on these texts, explains that when the mind dwells on vacant space without trees or any other concrete objects to anchor your mind upon, then the thought-constructs get absorbed in that void. And that is when the Light of

Divine Consciousness makes its entry and lets the aspirant know that there is a deeper Reality that is not open to the senses. As the boundary between the outer space and inner space is erased, the aspirant goes outwards and inwards simultaneously as another verse points out:

Sarvam jagat svadeham va svanandabharitam smaret/
Yugapat svamrtenaiva paranandamayo bhavet// 65

The *Yogi* should contemplate the entire universe or his own body simultaneously in its totality as filled with his (essential, spiritual) bliss. Then through his own ambrosia-like bliss, he will become identified with the supreme bliss.

This divine creative pulsation that stirs your body and mind is not just an abstract philosophical dictum, it is real and most immediate in this rarefied atmosphere. I felt so happy and carefree in that organic connection with my surrounding and in that haunting silence of the space I was singing the song of youthhood. Strangely, there was no feeling of loneliness in that solitude nor was there a need to share the joy with another fellow being. It seemed like an unselfish proprietorship or just an expected sense of belonging to nature. Here in this utter stillness of space and in the magic of raw nature, each one of us seemed to be at peace with the world and ourselves. Words are inadequate to describe these magnificent rock formations and the bright colours that fall over them. There are times when words turn out to be meagre and inadequate, it is best not to deploy them and this was one such moment. The vibrations from the atmosphere were satisfying enough and other than the drone of the Landcruiser engine, everything else was nature's sound. All of us in the vehicle effortlessly maintained silence;

we were just transfixed at the sight of the wondrous Tibetan plateau.

Our drivers kept an eye for each other's vehicles, and made sure that we were all within each other's view. The truck carrying all our essentials – tents, gasoline barrels, food supplies and our clothing etc., generally would be slightly delayed. In this bumpy terrain the truck takes longer to cover the distance. It was 5 P.M. and all the three Landcruisers came to a halt and our drivers and Sherpas decided to wait for the truck. After about 20 minutes all of them took a walk retracing our route in search of the truck.

For a while, the pause in our journey was interesting as some nomadic children flocked around us and they were puzzled and amused looking at their images on the video camera. These ragtag children appeared to have momentarily suspended their mud games and rushed to inspect our dust-covered jeeps and its occupants. In reality we didn't look much different either; even our bodies had several layers of mountain dust. We were charmed by their innocence and enthusiasm and they were intrigued by the equipment we had. The clock was running and there was no sign of the truck or our Sherpas and drivers and many of us were getting restless. The immediate cause was hunger. We had our breakfast cum lunch early in the morning around 10 A.M., and had no eatables to munch. Our fellow pilgrim Kailas *Behen* had a small packet of homemade crunchies and she generously shared it with all of us. From then on, I nicknamed her as 'our Annapurna' – the goddess with a potful of food and a ladle. Like the legendary *'Akshaya Patra'* – the mythical inexhaustible pot of food, her plastic bags seemed to contain a never ending supply of delicious snacks, but for now the larger supply was stocked in the truck, and we had to delight ourselves with a limited supply. This appetizer was enough to turn us ravenous and it was 6:30 P.M., and still there was no sign of truck, Sherpas and drivers. By now we had more to worry about than our hungry tummies.

This was our first open-air experience of the Himalayan dusk. The winds were blowing ferociously and the temperature dropped rather rapidly, and our heavy winter clothing was packed in the truck and not a single human body in sight. It was already 7:00 P.M., and pitch dark, and every passing moment seemed like eternity. It was almost 8:15 P.M. when our drivers and Sherpas returned looking very anxious. There was no sign of the truck and they walked as far as they could. In that darkness another small search team of 2 Sherpas and 2 drivers set out in one of the vehicles to find out the fate of our truck and we were left under the care of Ming Mar. At some distance there seemed to be a nomadic dwelling and we were taken to that modest shelter. Clearly, it was the dwelling of the nomadic urchins who flocked our vehicles earlier. The hostess was extremely gracious and she hurriedly prepared what seemed to be some version of noodle soup. Never before have I relished a bowl of some broth and noodles as I did that late evening.

Despite a contented belly my mind continued to be restless. The nagging concern about the truck lingered and with a bowlful of soup in my hands, feeling simultaneously grateful and tested, I chuckled at my own paradox. Perhaps this is to be expected; after all I am on my way to the home of the Lord who is the paragon of paradox. With a bowl in my hands, feeling and looking very much like a beggar, I have no choice but once again appeal to that '*Adi Bhikshuvu*' – the Primeval Beggar, who is none other than Shiva himself. Words of a fine Telugu poet, Sirivennala Sitaramasastry, whose lyrics became a popular film song, came to my mind:

> What does one ask that Primeval Beggar?
> The one who gives ashes, what do we ask him?
> To that fellow who has given only three days of life to the honey dripping flowery infants, what do we ask him?
> To that fellow who has given permission to huge boulders to live forever, what do we ask him?
> The god of love who facilitated his marriage to the daughter of the mountains was turned into ashes,
> To those haughty demons that have harassed the three worlds, he showed mercy.
> Flattery seeking elated Sankara!
> Three-eyed Lord! Short-tempered! Eccentric Sankara!
> What do we ask him?
>
> (Translated from Telugu by the author)

Right now stranded in the cold Himalayan night, this beggar seeks alms from The Primeval Beggar. The Lord of the universe who feeds the world is also the *Bhiksatana* – the wandering beggar. The idea of a 'giving beggar' seems to be an oxymoron. What is the god begging for? Clearly, statues of Shiva as the naked wandering ascetic begging for alms with skull in his hands are sculpted in the *Gopuras* (towers) of the Chidambaram temple. It is recorded in *Skanda Purana* that Shiva entered the penance grove of ascetics as a naked wandering beggar. On seeing his handsome body, the wives of the sages were seduced and they left all their chores behind and

The River Brahmaputra – 'the son of Brahma'.
This river was the guide to early explorers.

in the most irrepressible manner they exclaimed, "Only that lady is blessed who can freely and confidently embrace all the organs of the noble souled sage" (*Skanda Purana, Nagara Khanda*, 13-15). The sages angered by the lustful behaviour of their wives towards the wandering ascetic cursed that he be castrated. When Shiva's penis fell on the ground, mountains tumbled down, meteors fell and oceans overflowed. The other gods and demigods witnessing this extraordinary event realised that the *Lingam* is worthy of veneration. When gods appeal to Shiva, he said that he deliberately made these events happen to impart the secret of *Lingam* worship. Etymologically, the word *Lingam* has two roots – *'li'* means "to dissolve" and *'gam'* means, "to go"; together it means that *from* which the universe 'comes', i.e., created and that *in* which it dissolves. To impart this deep truth, he wanders into the forest as a naked ascetic, seducing chaste women and begging everyone to recognise deeper meanings. In his begging bowl he is willing to receive impulsive ignorance, illusions, inhibitions and vehement ego of his subjects.

My begging had only one meaning and one intent, "please clear the path and create no more delays." That night all of us huddled up in one small room, and altitude sickness took over and many suffered from severe headache, nausea and other digestive problems. It was the most unpleasant night and the only saving grace was when we heard the creaking noise of a truck coming to a halt around 2 A.M. Our truck had a mechanical breakdown and our driver could not go back and cross the checkpoint to get the necessary part. The Chinese officials were adamant about unwritten rules. Hence, our Sherpas managed to hire another truck, and transfer all the goods and reach us in that frightful darkness.

The pilgrims' path was never meant to be easy, and taking the safe arrival of the truck as yet another blessing we proceeded further the following morning. Life on the road, like life itself is tough and bumpy; there are all sorts of unexpected delights, setbacks, delays and dangers. Our guiding team seemed to accept it with equanimity that seems to emerge out of toughness and faith. I grew familiar with Kinna's oft-recurring slogan "*Problem* is our close friend", it is better to recognise this than to live in denial and fight a phantom battle with unknown forces. And so we headed towards our next camping site, somewhere near Zongba uncomplainingly, despite our unclean bodies and lack of toilet facilities, and above all altitude sickness that hit us at varying degrees.

We needed some distraction and thankfully we were greeted by the mighty Brahmaputra – 'the Son of Brahma' that flows all the way from Lake Manasarovar all across the Tibetan plateau and parts of North-Eastern India and Bangladesh before emptying out into the Bay of Bengal. This is the mighty river that has guided early explorers and its significance is mythical, historical and geographical. Its temperament also varies; it makes some regions fertile and very often floods other regions creating havoc. True to its name as the 'Son of Brahma' this river remains vital and majestic in time and space. Throughout the morning we dodged in and out of its sight and finally by noon crossed the Tamchok Khambab (Tibetan name for Brahmaputra) – the Horse-Mouthed River over a manually piloted ferry. After driving a couple of hours on those dusty tracks we finally reached our camping site close to a river brook.

I begged Ming Mar to construct some kind of an enclosure. I desperately needed to pour some warm water over my head and scrub my body with soap, to get rid of my splitting headache and get over the disgust with my dust-layered body. Ming Mar readily obliged and that was quite a relief. Nimma prepared sumptuous meals that night and we had an early satisfying supper and retired to our tents.

Inside the dark tent, I could hear the gurgling water of the brook nearby rise and fall according to some celestial rhythm, but its soothing sound did not put me to sleep right away. My rising curiosity prompted me to peek out of the tent a couple of times. The star-studded sky seemed so near that it practically blended with the landscape. If there was such a thing as plucking the stars, this was the moment. Only in fairy tales one has read about such shining stars in the dark sky. They were so playful and seemed to shoot straight at you and practically drop into your palms, and then suddenly vanish with a flicker. As tempting as it was to gaze into the dazzling sky, it was too cold to stay out and play with these celestial bodies. I crept back into my tent, but the stars were beckoning and again I crawled out. If the sunbeams falling over these mountains and vast spaces create colourful and scorching landscape that is so robust, the moonbeams present a beautiful black and white picture of the landscape, outlining the curves and folds of the hills, without any shadows or colours and yet making them clearly discernible. Even in this dark cold night I felt so nostalgic for it seemed like a memorable scene from an old film, perhaps with a melodious tune played out by a handsome hero and an enchanting heroine. Such close contact with celestial bodies does wonders to your soul. The smiling and shining stars so reassuringly tempt you to venture into the sub-conscious and dig out some pleasant anecdotes from the past – a song, a poem or a scene that has been carefully wrapped up in the memory storehouse so that by association the mind can register the present spectacle. The star-studded night even while being the subject of contemplation seems to instruct on the meaningful method of contemplation. The perceptual field guides you to appropriately record it into your conceptual field. It was too cold and windy to unzip the tent flap and peep out so many times and after a while just by sheer fatigue I dozed off for few hours.

Even before the crack of dawn, when the moon and stars are not visible and the sun has not risen, an extraordinary kind of diffused light pervades the landscape, making every hill seem so self-luminous. It is truly an astral light in all its naked intensity that makes the place glow. The soothing pastel colours of early morning with its cooling effect were perfectly suited for meditation. Furthermore, the rarefied air at high altitudes forces us to regulate our breathing – a built-in *Pranayama*, and plain walking becomes a conscious *'hatha-yoga'*, and when this is accompanied by rhythmic chanting, the effect is both tranquilising and energising. I realised that I was receiving a natural colour, sound and movement therapy and I immensely enjoyed being part of the living language of light and energy in motion. Colours and sound waves are supposed to be the hallmark of conscious perception and sensation and a touchstone of objective reality, but my subjective experience in this extraordinary

Lunch break on the Tibetan Plateau

Wading through the flowing streams
(Photograph: Courtesy of Duvvuri family)

atmosphere felt otherwise. I didn't know if I was a victim of hallucination, for everything looked topsy-turvy. Ordinary sensibilities show us that the sky is the source of light and the land is lit by it, but here the land exudes resplendency. Despite role reversals everything seemed to be in perfect harmony. It was a wonderful reminder that we are so organically connected to raw colours, pure sounds and perfect rhythms, and one cannot miss these mighty signposts on the Himalayan terrain. If one is attentive to these signs, they clearly navigate our life course, showing important milestones to be reached.

After dismantling our tents and loading all our baggage in the truck we proceeded to our next camping site. Our caretakers were ecologically conscious; our plates, mugs, and other utensils were stainless steel and therefore washed with the river water. If there were any disposable items like juice cartons, they carefully burnt them before leaving the campsite.

The journey was interesting; our vehicles practically waded through so many flowing streams. Heavens forbid, if these streams are swollen, they would practically bring the journey to a halt. Thankfully, *Surya Dev* (Sun God) was ever present and *Varun Dev* (Rain god) did not interfere. Our only contact with water was on the ground – the ever-flowing Brahmaputra meandering in and out of our sight. To our left at a great distance was the majestic Himalayan range serving as the marker between India and Tibet. It is a majestic crown shared by both the regions. The peak that stands out in the mountain range across the Indo-Tibetan border is Gurla Mandhata, standing at an impressive 25,350 feet. The Buddhists consider this mountain as the 'Head God' and thus the abode of their highest deity *Sangdul*. The mountain itself is one grand *Mandala* with concentric circles carved on the mountain face. We were awe-struck by its imposing grandeur.

We reached our camping site once again near a flowing brook by 5 P.M., and while the Sherpas were putting up the tents, I set out for a stroll, and very shortly some wild dogs surrounded me. They looked very ferocious and I felt robbed of my freedom. There was no point in venturing further, and having managed to leave the dogs unprovoked, I pulled myself away from the pack and returned to the safety of my tent. The previous night the celestial bodies enticed me into a wonderful game of hide and seek. But tonight, they decided to show a different character. Throughout the night, nothing could tame the roaring thunder and no one could silence the barking dogs. I wanted to get out and scream, "Shut up, I am going to see Kailash tomorrow", but the drizzling rain did not permit me to get out of the tent. When the celestial bodies beckon you to a fine game, you can yield, but if they goad you into a shouting match, it is best to resist and divert your attention. I concentrated on Kailash and built up my excitement.

EIGHT

THE GLORIOUS MOUNTAIN AND THE GRATEFUL PILGRIM

Being self – luminous
You cause everything to shine;
Delighting in your form
You fill the universe with delight;
Rocking with your own bliss
You make the whole world dance with joy.

You alone are the subject
Of their songs and speculations,
You, the subject of their quests and their worship.
Laudable, then, is the devotee's pilgrimage of life
Lived in harmony with you.
(Excerpts from Hymns 13 & 16 of *Shivastotravali* of
Utpaladeva)

The much-awaited day arrived, not as a slow transition
from its preceding stormy night, but as a day distinctly
apart. The sun was shining in abundance but there were
dark clouds at a distance. Intuitively, I did *Surya
Namaskar* (prostration to the Sun God) and chanted
hymns in his praise as a tribute. I knew this was the
day I wished and prayed for, but knew nothing of how

it would be and how I should be; a peculiar state of ignorance awakened and yet ignorant about anticipation. For months I rehearsed the moment, many a scenario came to my mind, and many a hymn I prepared to chant. But today, every type of rehearsed moment of rendezvous just disappeared from my conscious memory. I was really on the borders of the unknown, because the imagined world is just going to pale before the real. There must be some inevitable and invisible links in the cosmic sequences, and it is best not to guess various possibilities. Any *apriori* knowledge could be a hindrance, and hence I prepared to submit myself to the cosmic show.

The journey felt so prolonged on our now familiar undulatory path. My anticipation stretched along with the never ending mountain range and eventually just dissolved into vacant space. There must be a purpose for this dissolution of expectancy; for it keeps the element of surprise alive. I realise this as I am writing, but in the experiential mode, I was not even aware of the fact that expectation momentarily slipped out of my mind. I was not looking for some landmarks like rock cairns or flapping prayer flags. I was just lost in the present moment, enjoying every bit of my movement on this elevated stage on earth. Suddenly, like being jolted out of a slumber, I reacted to the 'turquoise stretch' ahead of me on the horizon and I exclaimed to our Tibetan guide,

"Dadu, what is that over there?"

"Mana...." Dadu murmured in a feeble tone.

"What?" I asked with a sense of urgency.

"Manasarovar, Manasarovar", he replied more clearly.

The first Darshan of Mount Kailash and Lake Manasarovar,
(Photographs: Courtesy of Dr. Chamraj Rao)

"Oh! My God! Oh! My God! That is beautiful"

I was stupefied. Last few days we have been riding alongside flowing waters. After all I was not in a desert chancing upon a mirage, or a real pond of water. Compared to this lake in front of me at a distance, the rivers and streams that we have seen were just enchanting, with all their zigzags and coils in varied colours. But what I see ahead of me is truly supernal. This is the heavenly lake created out of his mind by Brahma himself. The 'mind's lake' is in my vicinity and my mind and body are thrown into a hypnotic trance. Even before I could register this spectacle, our vehicle went down a ditch and quickly climbed over to a ridge and our driver pointed his hand towards the right. There was KAILASH! Yes, KAILASH! At a great distance but clearly visible. The pang and the palpitation that I experienced at that instant are inexplicable. Even before the vehicle came to a complete halt, I opened the door and ran in the direction of the mountain. I burst into tears, fell on my knees, down in a prostration, only to rise again and fall down to prostrate. I repeated this several times on behalf of all my family members. This instant, is the defining moment in my life. It gives meaning to my birth on this earth. Yes, I am seeing Kailash, in all its glory, completely uncovered, not a sliver of cloud obstructing my view. Glory to the mountain and gratitude to the white clouds! The thick clouds served as a backdrop to the mountain. The glowing whiteness of the mountain was clearly discernible from the relatively pale white clouds. The mountain is a perfect tetrahedron, smoothly covered with snow. In perfect symmetry, the mountain forehead is chipped in three horizontal lines at equidistance, giving a clear image of three horizontal lines of '*Vibhuti*' – ash marks characterising Shiva's face.

Blessed am I to get this view, blessed not because I am worthy of it, blessed because of Shiva's generosity. Just the previous night I agonised over clouds, storm and rain, and today in this cool mid-afternoon breeze, in perfect sunshine and clear skies, I see a magnificently decked *Lingam*. It looked like the heavenly priests have just concluded their ritual ablution – the *Abhishekam*, and perhaps did draw the cloud-screen to do their ornamentation – the *Alankaram*, and have drawn the curtain back just in time to offer *Darshan* to the eagerly awaiting pilgrims. The air was crisp and clean and once I spun around to get a panoramic view, it was overwhelming. There was the long stretch of turquoise blue waters between two glowing mountains – Kailash to the North and Gurla Mandhata to the South. This is the most precious jewel that nature can offer – a deep blue sapphire set between two lustrous diamonds. The diamond that I could not take my eyes off was the Kailash.

Scattered throughout India are innumerable shrines of Shiva, particularly in South India, the *Lingam* is gigantic and the temple *Gopurams* (towers) are intricately carved. These temples are the pride and glory of the *Chola* dynasty. But here, the mountain itself is the *Lingam* and all the adjacent mountains and hills that are so well chiseled and carefully hewn are the temple walls. Even from this spot, a huge rock facing Kailash looking like the hump of a bull, signifying Shiva's vehicle *Nandi* is visible. He is stationed right in front of his master. Here, Shiva is literally *Digambar* – he is only clothed by the sky. Conventionally, the temple towers are the ones that

The Southern face of Kailash. The mountain face is
chipped in horizontal lines appearing like
the ash marks on Shiva's forehead
(Photograph: Courtesy of Duvvuri Family)

the pilgrim first comes across, and then has to cross many barriers before reaching the sanctum–sanctorum of the temple to view the idol of the presiding deity. But in this natural shrine, no tower can encircle and envelop this Deity; all the surrounding mountains only surrender to this peak. Around here there is no room for individual glory, be it an emperor of a powerful dynasty, or an erudite scholar, or an evolved sage. Everybody becomes a humble devotee.

Witnessing this spectacular sight, I was reminded of my earlier immaturity. Just a few days back, when the Chinese held us up, I was so rash and vehement, and accused this father of mine of being negligent. I pestered him and dared him with such unabashed pride feeling so entitled. But today I am humbled. Few days back I presented my credentials and asked Lord Shiva to consider my application. Today, I realise that despite very few or hardly any meritorious acts on my part, I have been granted this extraordinary gift. I was ashamed and should seek forgiveness. But then to seek forgiveness for a recent aberration would be inadequate. My list of lapses is really long. Words from a traditional Hindi *Bhajan* (devotional song) express my shame:

Mailee Chadar Odeke Kaise, Dwar Tumhare Awoon,
Hey Pawan Parameshwar mere, Man he man Sharm Awoon.

Donning a sullied blanket, how do I come to your doorstep? Hey, the Pure Lord of mine, in my heart of hearts shame enters.

I stand here wrapped in a blanket that has accumulated so much dirt, so many errors, so many failings, and for which ones do I seek absolution? The devotional song rightly says, *"Janam Janam ke Mailee Chadar"* – 'the sullied blanket of many births' is what I am wearing. This hide has gathered so much filth that I am incapable of listing them. I once again fell on my knees and prostrated and wept uncontrollably, not because my shortcomings were glaringly visible, I knew that always, but because I got a clear *Darshan* despite my deficiencies. Under these circumstances, the *Bhajan* continues to capture my dilemma:

Man Veena Ki Tare Tooti, Ab kya Geet Sunawoon?
The strings of my heart's *Veena* have snapped, now what song can I sing?

It is relatively easy under ordinary circumstances to imagine the form of god and chant some hymns and sing songs. The melodic structure and lyrics give power to your imagination. But this rock pyramid, the throne of God is beyond imagination and leaves one speechless. Words and tunes seem inadequate and are even unavailable in this emotionally charged situation. In this initial overwhelming encounter, my prepared chanting was ineffectual. The fundamental law of aesthetics, a necessary distance from the subject of art is defied. There is only one consciousness, that of divinity, which is all encompassing and therefore only one act is possible – submission. I could only confess in all earnestness, "Hey *Bhagwan*, I need no greater proof that you are Compassion Incarnate, the fact that I stand here is a sufficient attestation".

There are so many laws, conventions and rituals that are defied here. It is customary to take some flowers, incense sticks and fruits when you go to the temple. But I came here empty-handed in every sense of the expression. Few days' back I suspected that God would send me back empty-handed, and today I stand here with no offerings except myself. The lyrics from the *Bhajan* once again capture this irony:

Hey Hari Har Me Harke Aya, Ab Kya Har Chadawoon?
Hey Lord, I come here defeated, now what garland can I offer you?

In the outburst of heavenly joy, this kind of defeat is not only accepted, but also rejoiced as the individual soul yields to the Divinity. At such an extraordinary moment when the soul opens itself to absorb the bliss, it seems too ordinary and mundane to chant routine *Mantras* or sing a song. I responded to this 'Godliness of Silence' with a mute prayer, silent gratitude and spontaneous submission.

Under the cloudless sky, on this balmy mid-afternoon, the prayer flags near me were fluttering in the cool mountain breeze, and a very revealing 'Silence' pervaded the atmosphere. My *Avva* – grandmother, when in a pensive mood would often hum a profound folk tune, and its gist is "In silence, in formlessness, in fullness, in calmness, like the ripening light beams of dawn uniting night and day, I discovered my Great Preceptor, *Shivoham*." I would playfully ask *Avva*, "how can silence be so godly", and she would playfully narrate a tale. Once upon a time four great sages – Sanaka, Sanatkumar, Saunaka and Sanatsujata were in search of a *Guru* who would teach them the method of self-knowledge. They first proceeded to *Vaikunta* and saw Vishnu relaxing on his serpent bed with one eye closed, while his consort Lakshmi was massaging his feet. On seeing this half-sleeping God in such splendour and comfort, they decided that a 'silent sleeping God' might not be able to impart the deep secrets of self-knowledge. Thus, they proceeded to Kailash, hoping that the dancing God would tutor them. Lord Shiva, anticipating the arrival of these sages, took the youthful form of *Dakshinamurthy* (the southern-faced god) and seated himself under a Banyan tree on the northern side of Lake Manasarovar. The sages saw Lord Shiva under the tree in perfect repose in a deep meditative posture. Silence prevailed. The vibration in the atmosphere was contagious and the sages also fell into deep meditation, and thus understood the method of spiritual contemplation. The moral of the tale is that silence is instructive as it clearly points out the method without wordy explanations.

I never understood then the power of silence that my *Avva* painstakingly tried to convey through simple stories. But today I viscerally experience its veracity. Sri Aurobindo has poetically penned about how profound truths are revealed in silence in his epic work Savitri:

> The genius of titanic silences
> Steeping her soul in its wide loneliness
> Had shown to her her self's bare reality
> And mated her with her environment.

(Book I Canto II)

When silence mates you with your environment, deep revelations occur. I stand before a magnificent mountain and an enchanting lake, and even from my vantage point it doesn't require a great stretch of imagination to know that the image of the mountain is reflected in the clear waters of the 'mind's lake'. In this simple geographical configuration is the 'Ultimate Truth and Method' – "Like the clear waters of Manasarovar, a clear mind reflects the God within." The task is to cleanse the mind, sharpen it, polish it and keep it free from fluctuations and when such a practice of Yoga intensifies, divinity can be seen within. Erudite scholars, great teachers, wise grandmothers and caring parents have hammered this lesson into us in so many ways. Today, in silence, I receive the same lesson from the Great Preceptor, *Dakshinamurthy* himself – a very effective 'show and tell' demonstration of Truth. The lesson is clear, pictorial and unforgettable.

Lord Shiva, in the role of a teacher is *Dakshinamurthy*, literally meaning, "Form facing the South." When the sages in the earlier tale went northwards seeking spiritual advice Shiva seated himself as a teacher under a Banyan tree facing southwards, and hence acquired the name *Dakshinamurthy* – the Great Preceptor. It is customary in temples and households to install their idols facing south. The seeker should go northwards to acquire knowledge and the one who imparts looks towards South. The first view of Kailash is its southern face. The lessons begin from the very first encounter. It is clearly explained in *Taittiriyopanishad* regarding the positionality of the teacher and pupil:

> *Acharya* (Teacher) *Purvarupam* (prior form looking South)
> *Antevasi* (pupil) *Uttararupam* (posterior form looking North)
> *Vidya* (learning) *Sandhih* (junction)
> *Pravachanam* (instruction) *Sandanam* (the means of joining)
> *Iti* (Thus) *Adhividyam* (on learning) *Dhyayet* (one should contemplate).

Taken together, the symbolic meaning is, the seeker

moves towards north for intellectual growth and the teacher facing south pulls the student to a higher level of knowledge. The directionality must be taken beyond the literal meaning, because the Sanskrit word *Uttara* not only means north, but it also means "that from which one has to go beyond". The great commentator Abhinavagupta of the school of Kashmir Saivism explains the various layers of meaning in his detailed exposition of Tantric Mysticism (*Paratrisaka – Vivarana*), and observes that the multiple meanings of the word '*Uttara*' appropriately fits the pupil's position and state of mind. He observes that '*Uttara*' may be interpreted as 'more', 'additional', meaning seeking more answers to additional questions arising in the mind. Abhinavagupta adds that '*Uttara*' also means 'speaking in a limited way' about Reality. Furthermore '*Uttara*' also means 'crossing over', i.e., *Moksha* or deliverance. Thus the word signifies the ignorant state of mind and also the process of liberating self from limited reality to unlimited or Infinite Reality. The 'crossing over' to the opposite and higher state '*Anuttara*' is facilitated by the spiritual guide who sets in motion his enlightened consciousness in the consciousness of the disciple. The capable teacher actualises the student's potentialities, and therefore there is nothing greater and holier than this partnership; it is even more sacred than the relationship between God and devotee. The fact that our first sighting of the mountain is its southern face signifying *Dakshinamurthy* – the Primeval Teacher, is symbolically significant and instructive. He alone can reveal some secrets hidden in this region. The great philosopher *Adi Sankaracharya* described the glory of this teacher in his beautiful Hymn to *Dakshinamurthy*:

To Him, who, like unto a magician, or even like unto a
mighty Yogin,
Displays by His own will this universe,
Undifferentiated in the beginning like the plant within the
seed,
But made afterwards picturesque in all its variety in
combination with space and time created by Maya,
To Him who is incarnate in the Teacher,
To him in the Effulgent Form Facing the South,
To Him (Siva) be this bow!
                    —Translation by Alladi Mahadeva Sastry

The first lesson to be learnt here is that, while what the naked eye sees is spectacular, the mind's eye must recognise that there is more than what meets the eye. The heights of Kailash are immeasurable for they are above and beyond all other worlds. It is said by Sage Sanatkumara to Sage Vyasa in *Siva Purana* that *Sivaloka* – the world of Shiva is even above *Satyaloka* – the abode of Brahma and *Vaikunta* – the abode of Vishnu. This is the residing place of the Universal Parents – Shiva and Parvati, and near this region is *Goloka*, where Mother Cows that feed the world reside. This place is beyond description as Sage Sanatkumara exclaims:

> Oh! Vyasa, Siva's region is wonderful and beautiful. It has no support. It shines with different objects. It cannot be specifically described. (Uma Samhita, Chap 19, 42)

According to *Siva Purana*, the earth's sphere consists of seven continents and seven oceans, and in the middle of all these is the continent *'Jambu Dvipa'* and at the centre of this continent is Mount Kailash, and therefore considered as the 'navel of the earth', the central 'axis' that holds the rotating world. It is both the centre of the world and the roof of the world and from this central high point the Universal Parents govern the world. After their marriage, Lord Shiva himself suggests to his consort Sati on the suitability of Kailash as their residing spot:

> Oh! My beloved beautiful woman, clouds will not reach the place where I have to make an abode for you.
> Oh! Comely lass! Even in rainy seasons the clouds move about in the side ridges alone of the Himalayas.
> Oh! Gentle lady, the clouds usually come only up to the foot of Kailas. They never go above it.
>
> (Siva Purana, Rudrasamhita, Section II,
> Chap. 22, 23-25)

Thus they took the peak of Kailash as their residence befitting the Primeval Couple. The heights of Kailash, free from the interference of clouds and rain, have been described by innumerable poets, since time immemorial in so many languages as an emblem of serenity. It has been described as a region that is *'Nirmal'* – tranquil, peaceful and harmonious.

According to the Buddhist tradition, seated at the summit of Kailash is the Great *Sakyamuni*, after conquering all the desires. The mountain blanketed with snow symbolises spotless purity of the Buddhist doctrine. This region is also the dwelling place of hundreds of *'Arhats'* – the enlightened beings who have annihilated all their passions and desires, and silently and invisibly emit spiritual vibrations for the benefit of other seekers. While the mountain symbolizes the immutable 'Absolute', the streams flowing at the foot of the mountain symbolise one's entry into the realm of 'Absolute'. The great poet / saint Milarepa describes Manasarovar as a 'green – gemmed Mandala', which is the 'fountainhead of four great rivers'. The water flowing into this lake is considered to be directly from the heaven and hence purifying and healing.

What is the meaningful lesson that one must receive having had the extraordinary opportunity to get to the foot of the mountain? Milarepa's response to this query is, the '*View*' from the mountain must clearly reveal the traps of Realism and Nihilism and these 'twin roads' must be shunned in order to reach 'Perfection's Road'. The resolution that must be made at the sacred spot is to discipline the 'misleading and wandering thoughts'. Finally one must put into '*Action*' the conquest of 'desire, debauchery and frivolity', till you reach the 'Pass of Freedom and Spontaneity'.

The greatness of Mount Kailash and Lake Manasarovar is axiomatic, even from this distant ridge. To heighten my experience, skies were clear, the clouds were co-operative and the mellowed sun rays of the mid-afternoon just perfect. It was like having a balcony seat at a grand theatre, witnessing a flawless show; the lighting is sharp and the acoustics just accurate. The recordings of early explorers, from Swami Pranavananda to Lama Anagarika Govinda were no exaggeration. Whether your affinity is towards Hindu scriptures or Buddhist literature, or both or neither, one truth is upheld; in the very first encounter, there is a valuable sermon at the foot of the mountain.

I don't remember how long I stood there in a hypnotic trance, quite unmindful of my mundane surroundings, till Kinna tapped on my shoulders and said gently, "*Lacchimi Didi*, let us go, we are going closer to Kailash", and he gently pulled me to the vehicle. As much as I wanted to prolong the magic of the moment, I yielded to Kinna's request.

I was awe-struck as we got closer to the mountain. I kept my head rotating in every direction to experience this multi-dimensional event. I felt eternally grateful to the 'White Clouds' for their generous cooperation in marking this special occasion. The mountain looked incredibly flamboyant against the backdrop of ethereal sky and an equally majestic lake at its foot. The contrast between the absolute 'blue' and 'white' in every direction made the spectacle truly surreal. When my vision was directed towards the vertical axis, I saw the deep blue sky above and the indigo lake below with the White Mountain suspended in between. When I shifted it to the horizontal axis, I saw the 'blue lake' in between two splendid White Mountains – Gurla Mandhata on one side and Kailash on the other. In this atmosphere saturated with splendour, everything seemed just perfect and justified. There is justification for the severance of this mountain from its main Himalayan range; it stands out alone and aloof, and unique from the rest of the world. It is a world in itself – the divine centre towards which the whole world gravitates. This is not a gateway to heaven; this is heaven. This is not the embassy of God's kingdom on earth; this is the kingdom.

Ironically, as we get closer to the foot of the mountain, there are stark reminders of earthly life. Human habitations appear, and the dwelling places look like they belonged to another era, with a string of mud houses surrounded by mud walls. Strangely, amidst these antiquated tenements one finds telegraph poles and power lines. It felt weird and strange seeing such signs of modern life in this otherwise antediluvian landscape. The anachronism disturbed my inner peace and I had to remind myself that I was in fact riding in a very modern day vehicle to this timeless spot. Once you come across series of Chinese army check-posts, you know with certainty that you are very much on this earth. As we approach *Darchen*, a tiny village practically at the foot of the mountain, we see numerous camping sites and along with that, other visible signs of modern day tourism – soda cans and juice cartons littered all over the place. All of us were visibly disgusted with so much filth in this sacred spot. I told Prema, "Heavens forbid, I hope there won't be a *Sheraton Kailash* here very soon, promising a balcony view of the mountain and the lake for a hefty price."

The guesthouse at *Darchen* was packed; there were many groups of pilgrims preparing for their *Kora*. Two ladies from another batch approached and asked me in Tamil,

"Will you be starting your *Pradakshina* tomorrow"?

"Yes, God willing", I replied and asked, "what about you"?

"Well, we have a problem", said one.

"What happened", I asked.

"Two elderly *Mamas*, from our group succumbed to altitude sickness and nobody knows what to do with their bodies".

"Oh! God! Were they in good health"? I asked.

"I think they lied about their age. Moreover *Mamas* from Madras have no idea of cold weather", said one lady and the other lady added, "they were unprepared and our journey....", and they broke down.

News about this unfortunate incident spread like wildfire within the compound walls of the guesthouse. Many opinions were exchanged ranging from physically unfit pilgrims venturing out to lack of screening by expedition companies causing great inconveniences and disappointments to fellow pilgrims. The commercial element in the pilgrimage seemed quite clear.

A pleasant and meaningful encounter at *Darchen* was with Swami Bikash Giri, who has spent twelve years in the Kailash – Manasarovar region and has done several outer and inner circuits of Mount Kailash. He also has published a pictorial account of his experiences in his book *Sumeru Parvat*. I was surprised to learn that this short, somewhat frail looking Swami has crossed the frozen Manasarovar, and circled Mount Kailash barefoot. Attributing this feat to the grace of the Lord of Kailash and his deep involvement in the *Tantric* tradition and Yoga, he emphasised the rigorous training of body and mind needed for spiritual adventures. The *Tantric* tradition deals mainly with magical and mystical formulations in the form of dialogues between *Shiva* (Spirit) and *Shakti* (Matter) on matters concerning creation, destruction, worship, attainment of super-human faculties and modes of union with the Supreme Spirit through meditation. I found our conversations with him extremely rewarding; he was a living example of the power of Yoga and Meditation.

The tiny village of *Darchen* is on the southern side of the Kailash peak, practically at the foot of the mountain. In Tibetan, '*Dar*' means '*Dhvaja*' or flag and '*Chen*' means big, hence '*Darchen*' means a big flagstaff of the nature's shrine. From the compound of our guesthouse one got a close-up view of Kailash without the hindrance of other connecting hills. It felt like being in one of the 'outhouses' in the 'side yard' of God's mansion. I drifted in and out of my room frequently to catch a glimpse of the mountain at different hours, trying to adjoin 'mortal time' with 'Timelessness'. No matter what the hour was, spiritual beauty illumined the atmosphere. At late afternoon, when the sunshine was at its brightest, the mountain presented itself as *Hemadri* – the golden peak and as it started cooling down it showed its silvery face – *Rajatadri*. The 'Great Time' synchronised with the beat of passing time, creating a continuum between the mortal soil and heavenly space. At each hour a different mood, but always in perfect harmony, the most beautiful and enduring partnership between the creator and the created. Each time I stepped out of my room, I stared at the mountain, amazed at its splendour. I would often stand there in a 'catatonic stupor', practically arrested in the Supreme Gaze, without any desire to be released from this kind of incarceration. With the passage of time, the reverential fear experienced earlier slowly transformed into familiar ease, comfort and a natural bonding. Feeling drenched in the calmness that prevailed in the atmosphere, I knew I had to rest my body in preparation for the *Kora* that is to begin the following day. I slept peacefully clutching the feet of that Great Dancer with my mind, body and spirit in proper alignment.

NINE

REVELATIONS ALONG THE
PILGRIM'S PATH

✞

Eternity multiplied its vast self-look
Translating its endless mightiness and joy
Into delights souls playing with Time could share
In grandeurs ever new-born from the unknown depths,
In powers that leaped immortal from unknown heights,
In passionate heart-beats of an undying love,
In scenes of a sweetness that can never fade.
Immortal to the rapturous heart and eyes,
In serene arches of translucent calm
From Wonder's dream-vasts cloudless skies slid down
An abyss of sapphire; sunlight visited eye
Which suffered without pain the absolute ray
And saw immortal clarities of form.

Sri Aurobindo's **Savitri**
(Excerpt from *The Book of Everlasting Day*)

Every step that I take the next three days to circle the
mountain is the most meaningful and essential step
towards 'The Life Divine' in this human journey. These
steps are not on even ground, but a gradual ascent from
an altitude of 15,000 feet to 18,500 feet and then the
descent to the plateau symbolising the difficult ascent

to spiritual heights and the necessary descent to the flat plains, bringing important revelations from the heights to the depths of human existence. Sri Aurobindo proclaimed emphatically that, "The ascent to the divine Life is the human journey, the Work of works, the acceptable sacrifice" and, "this alone is man's real business in the world and the justification of his existence, without which he would,be only an insect crawling among other ephemeral insects on a speck of surface mud and water which has managed to form itself amid appalling immensities of the physical universe." (*The Life Divine*, Chap. VI. "Man in the Universe"). Sri Aurobindo explains that for every step in man's ascension, there is a corresponding descent of the Divine; one movement matched by the other, the soul searches and the Divinity reveals in this wondrous play in the universe.

The celestial bodies offered their co-operation for this wondrous play and when our group was dropped off at the 'Mani wall' that marked the starting point of the *Kora*, the sun was shining brilliantly, the sky was blue, the clouds did not obstruct our view and the tip of Kailash was visible in full view. The guardian southern hills looked magnificent; they are undoubtedly the workmanship of a great sculptor and one sees more details of the majestic temple walls when the lens are zoomed. Against the immensity of this natural temple, our batch of pilgrims looked like tiny ants crawling in search of soul saving nectar.

Such close proximity to the sacred mountain produces an air of supernatural animation. A general silence filled the atmosphere, punctuated by the swelling and ebbing cadences of flowing streams. The

The Pilgrim's Path

great rhythm of nature pervading the atmosphere sets everything in motion and the pilgrim is drawn into it. Effort and imagination is no longer an individual fancy; one is an instrument of the same higher forces that govern the movements of the Sun, the Moon, the planets, the clouds, the oceans and the winds. There is no room for the 'I' in the steps that we take here. The slow and steady climb felt mysterious; some occult forces seemed to support every move or perhaps the Divine Parents have extended helping hand to their children struggling to take every small step. Quite early on in the *Kora* it dawned on me that this capital 'I' has no room here and that it has to be subsumed in the universal 'I'. This revelation came in a literal sense. Our caring Sherpa Nimma instructed me to take slow steps and offered to carry my rucksack to which I declined firmly, "No, no, I will carry". Before I could take ten steps, I realised the burden and even before I could make a request, Nimma came to my rescue. Clearly a voice from above is instructing me to shed expressions like, 'I can' and 'I will'.

The thirty-two mile circuit around Mount Kailash rises sometimes steadily, but very often abruptly from 15,000 feet to18,500 feet, where one crosses the Dolma La pass that symbolises the passage marking the transition from one life to another. It is the birth canal of the benevolent Mother, who forgives all our misdeeds and grants new life. The Buddhists call her *Dolma* and she is one of their most beloved deities, and for Hindus 'The Mother' here is called *Tara*, literally meaning 'She Who Helps Cross' to the other higher side of spiritual realisation. After the rebirth at the highest point on the circuit, the pilgrim descends to the plateau.

The passage of spiritual renaissance was to come the following day, and right now I had to concentrate on the present moment and absorb whatever vital energy I possibly could. The pilgrim's path runs westwards through a land of rocks, smooth pebbles and golden dust. To my left, the Barkha Plain unfurled as smooth wavy curves of earth, illuminated by sharp sunbeams and dappled by moving clouds. I could not however focus on this beautiful distant land. The inexorable exigencies of time and space required me to concentrate on the ground beneath and the high temple walls to my right, while I keep pace with other pilgrims. Every step appeared to forge a new link with higher forces and with the generations of devotees who have trodden the path. Countless heaps of stones lining the way is a clear testimony to their faith and determination—a reassurance for those who follow the path and also a verifiable truth that meaningful revelations are bound to occur along the way. My mother never gets tired of reiterating that one must follow the path paved by ardent devotees, for they alone can show the way. God is the goal, the destination, but the route can be shown only by the evolved souls, the *Bodhisattvas*, for their methods are valid and reliable and have stood the test of time. And so I walked along the well-trodden path keeping my *eyes* open to the signposts and the *ears* attentive to surprises that may come along the way.

The visual input was reassuring; my eyes were able to track the gigantic temple walls rising in regular tiers of horizontal ledges and their symmetry and architectural elegance was amazing. However the auditory input was unfamiliar for it practically sucks you into a void, and the more you strain and fine tune

The Yaks carrying the load

your ears, the feeling of nothingness heightens and with each step one is entering into an unknown realm. The silence deepens and intensifies as you walk; it is not quietness and tranquility in the ordinary sense that can be soothing, but it is a feeling of being swept into emptiness and tossed to dizzying heights of purity. My groping consciousness seemed so restful and calm in this soundless world. There was no searching and questioning contemplation, instead my mind was in an unusual state of equilibrium, fully convinced that this is an extraordinary world. It was not a sedated mind, but a mind opening itself to let the elemental life of cosmos to work its way through the sub-atomic cellular level of the body. Only when Gods shower their grace can one walk with the head held high. The fantastic rock formations carved by wind and water lining the high cliff demand that you look up and take steps. Like a carefree wandering child in some fairy tale, I walked along the high walls of the fortress wondering what the 'kingdom in the sky' on the other side would be like. With an almost voyeuristic impulse and childlike naivete and curiosity, I looked for some keyhole in the walls of the fortress hoping to get a glimpse of the city of gods, as I zoomed my camera lens to get few shots.

There was no need to stretch my imagination and curiosity about invisible icons for too long, as there were many interesting mythical emblems along the way. Standing at the western face of Kailash is a black hood-like peak and this is the *'Ravan Parvat'* named after the demon king Ravan. I find Ravan's relationship with Shiva fascinating; it is filled with intense devotion, audacity, playfulness and deceitfulness. Once Ravan went to the slopes of the Himalayas in order to fulfill a fierce vow and happened to see Lord Shiva with his consort Uma. Stunned by Parvati's irresistible charm, he was impudent enough to cast his left eye on the goddess lasciviously, for which the goddess duly scorched his left eye and turned his other eye grey, and hence one of his epithets is *Ekakshipingali* – one who has one eye turned grey (*Ramayan*, Uttar-Khand, Canto XIII 21-24). Despite such periodic censures his arrogance could never be subdued. He never hesitated to invite anybody's wrath, be it his brother, gods or his favorite deity Lord Shiva. Once he entered into a fierce battle with his brother Kuber (god of riches) and forcibly seized from him the *Pushpaka Vimana* – the magical aerial car and gleefully approached Mount Kailash in that splendid vehicle. The vehicle became motionless as it got closer to the mountain. Enraged by this obstruction, he put his hand below the mountain and lifted it up. Lord Shiva amused by his impetuousness and impressed with his strength sportively pressed the mountain with his great toe thus crushing the demon king's hand. In order to propitiate the Lord, Ravan composed a hymn eulogising the cosmic dance, and Lord Shiva being the hopelessly gullible God was flattered by these praises and presented the demon king with a shining sword known as *Chandrahasa*. (*Ramayan*, Uttar-Khand, Canto XIV). There are countless such tales of interesting encounters between Ravan and Shiva and each tale captures their dynamic relationship.

The hymn composed by Ravan with its cadenced lyrics can make one's soul leap out of joy, visualising the Great Dance:

The 'Ravan Parvat' at the southern face of Kailash

The western view of Kailash with broad flat rings
appearing like Saturn.

Jhatata Vi Galajjala Pravaha pavi Tasthale
Gale Va Lambye Lambitham Bhujanga Thunga Malikam
Dhama Dhama Dhamadha Manni Nada Vadda Marvayam
Chakara Chanda Tandavam Tano Tunah Sivah Sivam.

The sacred abode of roaring waters streaming down your forested braid,
With a neck from which hang coiled snakes
With *Dham Dham* echoes of *Dham Dham Dham* beat
Body rapt in whirling Cosmic Dance, Oh! Magnanimous Shiva.

The silence, the vastness, and the all round grandeur in the atmosphere was far too overwhelming for me to pause and chant the hymn. Although my lips failed to chant the hymn, my soul was able to fully feel its essence and I took delight in the kind of theatrical relationship that Shiva seems to invite from his subjects. I paid tribute to this enduring relationship with all its built-in contradictory forces as I passed along.

The patterns of snow formation on the mountain and the adjacent rocks present themselves as projective tests of pilgrims' inner world. With every step the design shifts like one grand nature's kaleidoscope much to the amazement of the viewer. For a stretch of time the western view of Kailash appears like Saturn, as the snow formation on the peculiarly shaped rocks resembles the broad flat rings circling the planet. From the same vantage point, when I reoriented my vision, the snow dispersal over the rocks looked like a sage with a long white beard in deep meditation. I didn't know if it was my subjective hallucination or an objective reality. Perhaps that debate was even irrelevant, since Mother Nature seemed to be administering Rorschach Test to detect the inner self.

After all, I was walking in the land ruled by the 'Lord of Actors', gaping at the face of the Great Dancer, and therefore it is to be expected that we simultaneously experience the polarities of the act and reality, the sublime and the ridiculous. The awe–inspiring mountain along with its adjacent hills forces the pilgrim to weave polarities to intensify the experience and recognise the wholesome nature of divinity.

There is no greater thrill than to see the footprint of the God embodied in The Great Dance. In the southwestern corner along the pilgrim's path we come across a huge *Shapje*—footprint on a rock. These dancing feet have been the object of veneration for innumerable sages and fellow-gods, and have inspired the most delightful hymns, lucid poems and profound philosophies of grammar and aesthetics, in addition to the aphoristic laws on Yoga. The movement of these feet is the very basis of *Natya Sastra* – 'the science of gesticulation and dance', and thus they preside over every pavilion of arts. The Lord of Dance who shows grace in his every move also shows perfection in stillness when in Yogic trance, weaving vitality and tranquility in body and mind.

Scriptures have recorded many tales of how the dancing feet have stimulated one too many incarnations and philosophical treatises. Once two students named Panini and Katyayana were studying under the able guidance of their Guru Upavarsha. While Katyayana seemed to possess extraordinary intellectual capabilities in comprehending abstract subject matter, Panini came across as shallow and dull-witted. Feeling disheartened by his limited learning abilities, Panini decided to perform penance and seek boons from Lord Shiva. As

Footprint of Lord Shiva

he wandered around to find a suitable place, he came across *Akshayabata* – the Eternal Banyan Tree under which many distinguished sages like Sanaka and Sanandana were performing severe penance and Panini joined them. Lord Shiva pleased with the dedication of all of them appeared as Nataraja and performed *Ananda Tandava* – 'The Dance of Bliss'. After the *Tandava* Lord Shiva played his *Damaru* – hand held drum—fourteen times. Upon witnessing this spectacular dance and listening to the beat of the drum, Panini realised *Maheswara Sutras* – the fourteen laws governing the philosophy of sound. Inspired by the rhythms of the dance and the drums Panini wrote *Ashtadhyayi* – the eight chapters of *Vyakarna Granth* – Treatise on Grammar, which to this day is the standard work in Sanskrit grammar. While Panini's work made his teacher very proud, it made his fellow student Katyayana burn with envy, and so he also performed penance and with the blessing of Lord Shiva wrote a commentary on *Ashtadhyayi,* known as *Vartika.* These verse commentaries are said to be an enquiry into *Ukta* – 'what has been said' and *Anukta* 'what has not been said', and *Durukta* 'what has not been said clearly', and thus Katyayana brought out all the omissions and commissions of Panini's work. The rhythms embedded in the movement of the Lord of Dance and the sounds emanating from his Damaru are the very basis for the natural cadences in Sanskrit recitation.

Rhythmic patterns are fundamental to our very existence; they are primary to our daily activities from breathing to walking to sleeping and they enable us to remember the arrangement of words in a poem or song. Rhythms can also make us forget the ordinary when they creatively configure time in music and dance in multudinous ways. Once Lord Vishnu while witnessing the Blissful Dance of Shiva lost in himself and became too heavy for Adisesha, the thousand-headed serpent to bear. When asked for the reason, Lord Vishnu said that he was so captivated by the Dance that he forgot himself, and this response kindled Adisesha's interest who performed a penance and was born as Patanjali on earth. It was he who composed a hymn called *Sambhu Natanam* while witnessing the Glorious Dance in *Chidamabaram* – 'sky of consciousness'. The hymn captures not only the ecstasy of rhythm in the majestic dance, but also the thrill experienced by the assembly of Gods who came to witness the show as evident in the stanza:

> *Ananta – navaratna – vilasat – kataka – kinkini – jhalam – jhalajhalam- jhalavaram*
> *Mukunda – vidhi – hastagata – mardala – layadhvani – dhimiddhimita – nartanapadam*
> *Sakuntaratha – barhiratha – nandimukha – bhringiriti – sangha – nikatam*
> *Sanandana – sanaka – pramukha – vandita padam – para chidambara natam hridi bhaje.*

> Sambhu Natanam by Patanjali. Translation and Commentary by H.H. Swamini Sarada Priyananda. Chinmayaranyam

Adore in the heart, the Lord whose bracelets studded with nine jewels and tiny bells continuously making *jhala jhala* sounds, whose feet are dancing making *dhimi dhimi* sounds in rhythm with the sounds of the drums in the hand of Vishnu and Brahma, who has the crowd of Vishnu with the bird chariot, Nandi, Bhringi near Him, to whose abode salutations are given by Sanaka, Sananda and others.

To those feet adored by all deities and sages, I prostrated

Elephant shaped rock with all the details
in the south – west corner

while my inner ear heard some of these rhythms. Patanjali not only captured the movements of the cosmic dancer, but also captured the Lord in stillness and compiled *The Yoga Sutras* – the maxims on Yogic practice, so widely used in every Yoga school to this day.

The magical moments along the *Parikrama* circuit seemed inexhaustible. Soon after crossing the footprint on the ground my attention was once again riveted to the high mountains. A peculiarly shaped rock appeared on an adjacent hill at what seemed to be the base of Mount Kailash. I could neither take my eyes off this rock nor could I decode its shape. From certain angles it looked like the hood of a cobra, an interpretation that seemed plausible. After all, when Shiva wandered around as a naked beggar in the pine forest seducing chaste women, the angry sages dispatched their sacrificial Tiger and Cobra to attack him. Shiva in turn tore the Tiger's skin and wrapped it around his waist, and wore the cobra as a garland around his neck. As I walked along further, the hooded cobra shape started fading and the rock was beginning to look like a huge animal comfortably seated at the foot of the mountain. I tried to reorient my perception several times to make sense of the rock, and after few more steps, everything was crystal clear. It was a huge elephant shaped rock with all its details – huge ears, tusk and even the folds in its thick shining hide. No sculptor could have shown so many details. This was the most magical and unexpected moment of my pilgrimage. My extensive research prior to this journey did not prepare me for this moment. In my mind it was a clear *Darshan* of Lord Ganesh, the elephant headed son of Lord Shiva and goddess Parvati, although the elephant could signify other things. Is it Kuber, the god of riches and a friend of Shiva who made his home at the doorsteps of Kailash or is it one of the *Yaksha*, demigod, guarding the wealth of Kailash? Or is it Indra's elephant *Airavat* that has taken a trip to Kailash? The symbolism is purely in the eye of the beholder and in my view it was young Ganesh seated at the feet of his parents, and as a principal attendant guarding the inner chambers. Lord Ganesh is the remover of obstacles, and passing by this rock felt so auspicious and blessed. Furthermore a convention is upheld; in any temple no matter who the principal deity is, it is customary to first pay obeisance to Ganesh before approaching other idols, and even in this grand nature's shrine, very early on, in the south-western corner, Vinayak, the remover of obstacles appears before our eyes. With so much grace shown with great clarity with an added element of surprise, I cannot ask for any further proof of divine play. Such pleasant encounters do wonders to your soul; my body and spirit felt light as if unburdened of some unnecessary weight. When the majestic elephant God is by your side, one can and should be carefree. This magic sustained me for the rest of the trek and I reached the camping site at the northern face to experience more mystical phenomena.

The northern face of Kailash is beyond description – a celestial temple with a dome of gold and silver studded with diamonds and guarded by equally majestic hills in varying shades of dark brown colours, sharply contrasting the mountain to support its radiance. The mountain seemed so near, almost tempting one to walk over and touch it, and yet its heavenly grandeur made it beyond the realm of human touch or words. It is no exaggeration that Lama Anagarika Govinda described this as, "the seat and centre of cosmic powers, the axis or hub which connects the earth with the universe, the super-antenna for the influx and outflow of spiritual energies of our planet" (p.215). This super-antenna is undoubtedly an amplifier of spiritual experience. While the southern face as *Dakshinamurthy* – the teacher is benevolent and beckoning, the northern face shows God's cosmic energy and power. Its pristine beauty, its illusory nearness and its towering height are absolutely astonishing, and a million prostrations cannot be a fitting tribute to this perfection.

The two hills on either side of Mount Kailash are *Vajrapani* and *Manjusri* in Tibetan mythology. *Vajrapani* is the 'Wielder of Diamond Sceptre' symbolising the indestructible weapon to fight Darkness and Decay, and *Manjusri* is the patron saint of active learning and wisdom. Right next to *Manjusri* is the hill of *Avalokitesvara*, the Boddhisattva of compassion who attentively listens to the grievances of the seekers and conveys them to the Sakyamuni Buddha. As a compassionate saint his gift to humanity is the famous Mantra, *'Om Mani Padme Hum'*, and with this he has shown the world the path to Enlightenment. A hill adjacent to *Vajrapani* on the north-eastern side is said to be born out of Avalokitesvara's tears and it is the hill of Dolma – the benevolent mother who absorbs all the misdeeds and sanctions new life to the seekers. The kingdom of God seemed so well assembled with these four hills standing on either side of the mountain as guarding sentinels.

The grandeur only intensified as evening fell and gradually the region was enveloped by darkness. In that pitch dark region there was only one shining object revealing its splendor with all the details of its symmetrical contours. This was the most extraordinary night of my life; I was a woman possessed by some supernatural powers that revealed some simple truths in the most profound manner – *In the dark world there is only one Power that is self-effulgent, follow that light, and that alone can lead you from darkness to brightness.* The mountain seemed to radiate at the top, in the middle and at the bottom effusing astral light all around. The depths from which the light is emanating is beyond anyone's comprehension and the heights that my naked eyes can see is only the sub-structure of something more grand and limitless. At this remarkable hour one of my *Avva's* tales came to my mind. She would effortlessly make this story filled with humour, folly and wisdom, all so magical.

Once upon a time, Lord Shiva out of compassion and tenderness and with a sole intent of imparting a valuable lesson to his subjects rose as a Column' of Fire filling the chasm between heaven and earth. The splendour of the Fiery *Linga* made everything around look so pale and all the planets along with the galaxies of stars shone as never before. It is recorded in *Skanda Purana* that both Vishnu and Brahma became curious, anxious and competitive to measure its heights and they pondered thus:

From whom has this come out? What is its root? What is its place of origin? What is its base? By which power does it shine?

What is its extent all round, sideways, above and below?

How far has it gone deep into the nether worlds?
The mind is constantly eager to know all this. It appears to
fly up in the sky and penetrate deep into the nether world.
(*Skanda Purana*, Maheswara
Khanda. Uttarardha, Chap. 10. 21- 23)

To discover its dimensions, Vishnu took the form of a
boar and penetrated through the earth and Brahma took
the form of a swan and flew up towards the sky. Vishnu
penetrated far beneath the oceans and yet could not see
the roots of the column of light and admitted his
inability. Brahma on the other hand was blatantly
perjurious, and found an alibi in *Ketaki* flower that was
falling from unknown heights, and together they lied
that they have seen the heights of this shining column.
Angered by this deceit, Shiva pinched off Brahma's fifth
head and proclaimed that *Ketaki* flower for giving false
evidence shall never be used to worship him. After
realising the power of the Column of Fire, Brahma and
Vishnu along with other gods eulogised Shiva.

What I saw before my eyes was the physical
manifestation of that Column of Light and I spent hours
late into the magical night transfixed to this wondrous
mountain, quite unmindful of Kinna's instructions to
have a good night sleep in preparation for the eventful
day ahead. At that hour I could not imagine anything
more resplendent and ornate than what I was
witnessing. It was impossible to shut my eyes and each
time I tried to force some sleep I failed. My eyes wanted
to see more. To heighten this effect, almost as a playful
reward for staying up late, the beautiful crescent moon
perched itself on the left side of the mountain revealing
Shiva as *Chandrasekhar*, the Lord adorned with the
crescent moon. Myths have recorded innumerable tales

on the relationship between the moon and Lord Shiva that are beyond the scope of this narrative. The cooling and soothing effect of the moon is the antidote to Shiva's angry persona.

The appearance of the moon had a cooling and calming effect on my excited mind, and its gentle nature was enough of a lullaby to put me to sleep for few hours on that eventful night.

TEN

THE DOLMA LA PASS:
EPIPHANIES AND REBIRTH

*Om Triyambakam Yajamahe Sugandhim Pushtivardhanam
Urvaarukamiva Bandhanaat Mrtyormuksheeya Maamrtaat.*

We worship Lord Shiva the three-eyed one, the one who is
the master of all senses and qualities and the one who is
the sustainer of growth. May he release us from the bondage
of death as a ripened cucumber is released from its stalk,
and may he grant us immortality.

> (Rig Veda, Maha Mrityunjaya Mantra – the Great
> Mantra of the Lord who conquers Death.

*Na Jayate mrityate va vipascit
Nayam kutascinna babhuva kascit
Ajo nityah sasvatoyam purano
Na hanyate hanyamane sarire*

The knowing soul is not born, nor does it die. It does not
come into being from anything, nor anything has come into
being from it. The unborn, eternal, everlasting, ancient One
suffers no destruction, even when the body is destroyed.

> (Kathopanishad, Chap II, 18. Lord of Death – Yama's
> response to Naciketa's query on death)

The northern face greeted dawn as gracefully and gently as it bid farewell to night, slowly changing its face from a silvery glow (*Rajatadri*) to a golden glow (*Hemadri*). Time passes by the mountain every moment, seasons pass by the mountain every year, pilgrims pass by the mountain occasionally, all of them bound by the rhythms of the cosmic dance, everything changes, most of them transient, but what remains forever is the mountain and its glow. The passers-by are lit by this glow, energised by its powers, carry the fragrance, register the image, record the sounds, receive sacred offerings and bow to its grandeur. Lama Anagarika Govinda is right; one must see the mountain, particularly the northern face at different times in different seasons to experience its moods and appreciate its greatness. My fellow pilgrims and I have been fortunate enough to see the dusk fleeting by and darkness set in only to be gently pushed by dawn in preparation for the day. These significant hours have been intense enough to penetrate deep into my soul and leave lasting impressions not only for a lifetime but also for many more lives to come. Even as the sunrays have been warming up a few patches of the land, it was time for us to set out on our trek for the climactic moment of our pilgrimage.

This is the day that we have been cautioned several times by just about everybody who has undertaken this pilgrimage, be it in recent or distant past. Early on in the trek, it was crystal clear that there are many hills to be climbed, many gushing streams to be crossed on make-shift rickety bridges, many dangers to be escaped and many gracious moments to be thankful to, and this day is 'THE DAY' in the journey of consciousness. It is

The Northern face of Kailash Rajatadri – the silvery glow

a day in which one must swiftly slide between different realms of reality. There is the reality of the body's limited capacity, the feeble will power of the mind, the fixed Divine plan, the unyielding demands of the rough terrain, and all these different realms erase the boundaries between the ordinary and the extraordinary. As the trail moves upwards steeply, the veil separating the real from the surreal, belief from truth, fact from legend wavers and is finally blown away.

After scaling several hills, when I became consciously aware of all metaphysical barriers melting away, I had one of the most amazing rapturous moments to mark the occasion. With the able assistance of my Sherpa Nimma, I was a bit ahead of my fellow pilgrims and Nimma asked me to pause and halt, while he assisted others. This was a good opportunity to give some relief to my heaving lungs and so I sat on a near-by rock, still damp with morning dewdrops.

I saw many more hills in my vicinity to be climbed and the Sun was slowly rising behind those hills, turning the sky gradually into bright orange, but those mellowed sunrays hadn't reached the region I was in. It was one grand spectacle unfolding before my eyes; while I was enjoying the early morning cool mountain breeze, I could feel the slowly rising warmth of sunshine behind the hills. Almost unexpectedly, a Buddhist monk in dark burgundy robes passed by me and very quickly turned his face and looked straight into my eyes and uttered '*Om Mami Pemme Hum*' and walked away briskly towards the hills. Despite the fleetingness of that greeting, I was able to register his very sharp features on a well-chiseled face and there was a husky depth to his voice. He walked away with a great sense of urgency, as if he was rushing to conduct some god's business. And even before I could recover from this brief vigorous encounter, he was already ascending the hill and all I could see was the silhouette of a handsome human body against the backdrop of Mother Nature's grand plan. The monk's burgundy gently blended with the bright crimson red sky in the background, and as the body moved on the hill, everything turned into a grand display of man's relationship with nature. It looked as if Mother Nature was holding her son to her bosom and was proudly flaunting her creation. As I sat there marvelling at this picture-perfect sight, the melodic tunes of a classical composition of Saint Tyagaraja "*Hari Dasulu Vedale*" in Raag Yaman Kalyani reached my phantasmic ears, and the song goes:

> The servitors of Hari (God) set out
> Delightful was the sight
> Joyous was the feeling
> The servitors of Hari set out.

> Chanting Hari Govinda, Hari Rama Krishna
> Reciting the names in sequence
> Uttering them with tenderness
> The Servitors of Hari set out.

> With wisdom, singing the song
> Meditating on Rama and receiving good alms
> The servitors of Hari set out.

> Spraying fragrances on the King of kings
> Making everything lustrous
> Tyagaraja along with the servitors of Hari set out.
>   (Saint Tyagaraja. Translated from
>   Telugu by the author)

This delightful composition – one of my favourite, both as a performer and as a listener has in the past produced many moods and sentiments within me. I have sung and heard many variations of this piece and have imagined many a scenario to match the lyrics. I have imagined a procession of *'Bhajan Goshti'* – a group of devotional singers passing by in the streets in the early morning hours singing melodious tunes and being awakened by it. This is a common practice in many parts of India, and this was always a treat to all our senses. I have imagined celestial choir gliding in the skies with their musical accompaniments, enthralling the earthly beings. Every image that came to my mind over the years, I felt was inadequate, convinced that Saint Tyagaraja must have had a different picture in mind. But today, at the most unexpected moment, in the most extraordinary setting, when all the sensory inputs are so pleasant, the scene is presented to me like a gift. I don't know which heavenly minstrel is rendering the piece; I heard all the nuances in the melodic structure set to perfect rhythm and infused with intense devotion. In this place presided by none other than *Nada Brahmam* —the Sound Manifest, the acoustics are perfect, the architectural grace of the concert hall is grand, and the performance is flawless. My soul simply had to yield to rapture's call and fully absorb all that my clairaudience could receive and just be awakened to this unearthly wonder and delight. In any life's tale there can only be a few such epiphanies, when one can tune the finite with the infinite and the body's rhythm synchronises with the celestial rhythm. In ordinary concert halls, a rendition by even the most talented singer could only produce a normal scene, which of course is attributed to my limited clairvoyance. But today a monk climbing the hill in the early morning hours chanting mantras brought the sounds that were inaudible to my deaf mortal ears to life. Was it his mantra that made me so clairaudient? After all, all the seven musical notes are contained in that single syllable *Om*. As the monk reached the high point on the hill, the musical notes reached a crescendo and the lyrics swelled into a canticle and I had a taste of ecstasy.

Inasmuch as I wanted to prolong the waltz with the Unknown, on the valley floor, it was time to move on since the music stopped and the monk was getting out of sight. I must now follow his footsteps and resume the ascent over huge granite boulders. As one approaches the eastern corner, in the *Polung Chhu* (literally meaning incense valley), Kailash presents itself as a giant silver '*Shiva Linga*' placed on an intricately carved pedestal. A glacial arm stretches out from the main peak up to the adjacent Jambyang peak. This horizontal conglomerate, in perfect proportion extending from the mountain presents one with the familiar image of *Lingam* in the temple. The smaller adjacent peaks serve as pedestals doing justice to the panorama. From the pilgrim's path it looks like a gigantic icy pyramid with a stem floating in the air. This view disappears as suddenly as it appears - a game that heaven seems to play; suspend an apparition along the way and pull it away immediately. On a realistic plane one cannot pause and rejoice in the spectacle. By this point, the ascent is getting steeper, the altitude higher, the air thinner and breathing indeed a struggle, and there is a great sense of urgency to reach the Dolma La Pass by early afternoon. At that high exposed point,

The Northern face of Kailash Hemadri – the golden glow

a blizzard can hit unexpectedly and freeze a person in a matter of few minutes.

Before reaching the high Dolma La Pass one must pass through the gates of death, and in this land stretching close to five kms, ruled by Yama, the King of Death, one must face judgement, rid the body and soul of past misdeeds, before one is awarded a new life atop the Dolma La. With every step I took on this shrouded path, I felt I was walking into the heart of mystery. My energy level was depleting steadily, only to be revived by occasional whiffs of oxygen provided by Sherpa Kinna. The eerie feeling was overpowering; it felt like the soldiers of Yama's kingdom have lined up the path ready to throw the noose. There was only one protective sheath that I could invoke—chant the five-syllable mantra *Om Namah Sivaya*. This mantra organised my every step and my every breath. The duration between inhaling and exhaling and lifting one foot and placing it few inches ahead was filled with the murmur of *Om Namah Sivaya*. *Om* ... inhale ... lift right foot ... *Namah Sivaya* ... exhale ... place the foot forward. *Om* ... inhale ... lift left foot ... *Namah Sivaya* ... exhale ... place the left foot forward. This circular reaction continued. I had to wrap myself in this mantra and that was the *ONLY* way to dodge the attendants of Yama.

This is the only mantra that can repel the all-enveloping death, and that's why one of Shiva's names is Mrityunjaya – Conqueror of Death. There are innumerable tales to attest to this power, and one such well-known story is about young Markandeya, who was born to Sage Mrikandu and his wife Marudwati and he was sanctioned only 16 years of life. On the destined day Markandeya went to the Shiva temple and embracing the Shiva Linga, immersed himself in deep meditation and worship. When Yama, the Lord of Death came to take the boy's life, he saw that the boy was inseparable from the Linga and thus cast his lasso around the boy's neck along with the Linga. Shiva appeared in his angry form and kicked Yama with his foot, thus granting Markandeya immortality.

In this stretch, presided by *Yama* every gasp of breath that I took seemed to be a gift from above. Every breath was supported by a drop of elixir from heaven. I am consciously aware of this ability and inability to breathe for this has been the defining moment of my life story and my point of contention with this Father in Heaven. At a stage in life when I wanted all the promises of life to be handed to me, I saw the stark reality of death. Yes, Death, right before my eyes. I saw and heard the first cry of my father late one night when Yama approached him. My father called out my name in desperation and in pain and the Myocardial Infarction took over. I stood there helplessly as the noose was tightened and to my horror my father was fighting to breathe the last few minutes and finally I saw him take his last breath. The struggle with *Yama* was all over. I know that exact moment which has been recorded in my body's clock. Since then many battles have been waged with the Lord of cremation grounds (Shiva) and right now I am in *Shiv Tsal*, where I must shed my baggage, my fears, my anger and my misdeeds and pay homage to the departed souls. It is time to pause and pay tribute to my father and my grandmother.

Shiv Tsal: Remembrances of the departed souls

All these years, my conversations with THE FATHER about my father were fraught with anger, agitation,

Kailash appears as a giant silver 'Shiva Linga'
on an intricately carved pedestal.

blame and finally sadness. Today, on this high purgatorial cremation grounds in this in-between land, the early emotions came to a stand still – a state of emptiness and nothingness with no questions to ask and no disputes to be settled. I was neither a thinking nor an emoting subject, but just a viewer, as images from my father's life flashed before my eyes. I saw the satisfied look on his face when the All India Radio played a song of K.L. Saigal. I saw his nod of approval and appreciation when he heard Parveen Sultana's *Khayal*. Much to my embarrassment as a teenager, any reference to Parveen Sultana had to be followed by my father's fascination with her beauty. To him a performance by her was an audio-visual treat. I saw him bouncing at the very mention of Bade Ghulam Ali Khan, and his voice practically made him blithesome. I saw the reverential face when he heard the voices of Ariyakudi Ramanuja Iyengar and Semmangudi Srinivasa Iyer. I saw him deeply immersed in James Boswell's narrative of Samuel Johnson's life admiring the beauty of English language. When he came across an interesting passage, he would call out for me and I would have to suspend all activities to listen to him read the passage aloud and over the years I have heard practically the whole book. All those years I never could understand a biographer's adulation for his subject, all the same just to please my father I sat and listened to the narrative attentively. I saw him burst into hysterical laughter meeting P.G. Wodehouse's character Mr. Jeeves. The scene at my family dinner hour appeared; my father would attempt to deliver a joke, except there was one problem, he would laugh uncontrollably before delivering the punch line. The laughter was infectious enough and all of us joined him sometimes not knowing what we were laughing about. When he came under the spell of music, even at the most unusual time, all other activity had to come to a halt; midway through his shaving ritual he would pause and spontaneously render a musical version of *Shiv Tandava Stotra* – Hymn in praise of the Cosmic Dance. So casual was the setting, and yet so intense and powerful was the rendition. I remembered one instance when pillion riding on his scooter to my college, we heard the radio from one household playing K.L. Saigal's song *"Gham diye mustaquil, Kitana najuk he dil, Yeh na jana, Haye haye ye zalim zamana"* (Sorrow is given perpetually, how delicate the heart is, I did not realise, Hey, hey, the ruthless world). My father abruptly came to a halt and we stood at their compound wall and heard the song and then proceeded. He remarked about how enchanting melancholy could be. I also remembered the time when I lost his Sheaffer pen that had a gold nib and faced his ire. My father treasured pens, books, music albums and carelessness with any of these things was intolerable to him. Only a man wedded to all aspects of Goddess Saraswati (incidentally, my mother's name) from words to musical notes to written notations can attach such sentimental value to these things.

Today my life revolves around libraries, concert halls and theatres and I understand the worth of these places. My father never preached about the wonder of music or the power of great books; his passionate engagement with them simply revealed their grandeur. In every activity that I engage in I feel my father's presence, hear his words, and am watchful to the ethical compass held by him. More years have been spent in his absence than in his presence, and yet as time passes by I feel a lot closer to him and have more lively discussions with him. The resident of this mountain alone knows the pain that my father's demise has caused me. Yet, strangely enough, as I behold the Mirror of the King of Death on this high cremation ground, I see life affirming images before me. As I struggle to breathe while passing through the gates of death, I realise how *ALIVE* my father is. He must be in this region, having joined the celestial choir, enjoying every moment to the fullest. In the Land of Death, if I can experience forces of Life, there must be a subtle message—some spirits do not just vanish, they simply take on a different form. My realisation of this truth is a daughter's tribute to her father—for this legacy my eternal gratitude to my father/Father.

No ritual of death is complete without the invocation of one's *Gotra* – lineage. There are no officiating priests here and no rituals to be conducted. Still, I must state my lineage to pay tribute to another extraordinary individual in my life. My lineage is forked involving two grandmothers held together by a pact with Lord Shiva. My father was the youngest son in a large family. My paternal grandfather was a physician and his patients got additional care from my grandmother. My paternal grandmother was a strong willed woman, who had a mind of her own and was quite radical for her times. More importantly she was known for her charitable nature. My grandfather earned and she donated. In her view the sick patients needed more than medication, and hence to the mal-nourished she fed them *Dal rice* with ghee followed by curd rice and to the ones suffering from leprosy and other skin conditions, she gave them soothing herbal oil bath. She sincerely believed that she was answerable to her favourite deity, Lord Shiva. She also built a temple for Lord Shiva in our village Gudur, in Andhra Pradesh. When my father was very young, he fell seriously ill and at that time she made a pact with Shiva that if he survived, she would give him up for adoption to a childless couple. The deal with Lord Shiva worked and my father was formally adopted by my grandfather's niece and her husband who were childless. In short, my father was adopted by his cousin sister and her husband. Since the adoption took place within the family he had the benefit of parents on both sides.

I did not know my biological grandmother; she died a year before I was born and hence named after her. Everything about her nature I learnt from my adopted grandmother, my beloved *Avva*, who needed a family to love and children to listen to her stories and her music. My siblings and I were the recipients of this unadulterated love. My *Avva's* family tales depicted a heroic image of my biological grandmother – her generous nature, her outspokenness and her intense devotion. One grandmother gave and the other received; both knew their roles. One never mentioned about giving, the other never forgot what she received. Together, theirs was a tale of Gift and Gratitude; neither of them asserted proprietorship and neither one of them shirked responsibility. This is my lineage.

To tell even a short story of a woman who excelled all other great storytellers known to me is a presumptuous task. But at this juncture, on this very sacred spot in *Shiv – Stal*, failure to do so would be a betrayal of love. I must show gratitude to a woman who

Pausing at Shiv Tsal with Sherpa Nimma

personified gratitude. For twenty-five years of my life, I slept right next to her, and practically every night she entertained me with bedtime stories. Every tale of hers generated another tale, and she would intricately weave family tales with historical and mythical tales. She was at once the teller and performer becoming the microcosm of creating divinity. The clarity of her narration and the elegance of her language (being a polyglot she would switch codes to produce the needed effect), and the theatrical effect of unfolding plot kept me, along with my siblings completely enraptured. She built many fantasies, imaginary worlds and endless possibilities for interpreting every character in their thickening plot. Her *tale* and her *tales* are inexhaustible.

But her story and my story have a tragic chapter. She lost her son and I lost my father. It was unnatural for her and untimely for me. After my father's demise she would lament about the deep irony in the pact she made with Lord Shiva. She said her husband needed a son to light his funeral pyre, whereas she desperately needed a son and his family to love. Both got what they wanted, but she also got what she neglected to state in the pact. No one ever thought that a pact with God would have literal clauses underlined.

With so many colourful chapters in her life, her **Gods** were an interesting bunch of characters. They were so real, so familiar, so human and yet so divine. Like a great teacher of literature, she enticed us into loving her characters. It was difficult to resist; God came packaged with her love. Every night depending on the day's event or my mood she picked the most appropriate tale and narrated with intensity while gently stroking my hair with her soft wrinkled hand.

There was a message, an answer, and a solution to my current predicament. God was not the authoritarian examiner of my life, but a great character to suit my various needs and moods. She showed variety in Gods, their humanness, their deceptive strategies and their power and grace. Over the years I can't think of God without grandma and grandma without God. They are a package deal. Her Gods were sexy, funny, adorable, and most importantly relevant to daily life. There was no hypocrisy in her practice. The ultimate renunciation came towards the end of her life. We were in the process of filing immigration papers to the United States and were struggling to come to terms with her care. She encouraged us to seek our future and not be burdened with her well-being. She said even Rama, her favourite god had to renounce his love and nobody is spared of adversities. She said her love was meant to set us free. It was never meant to be duty bound in her view. She had to be left under the care of my cousins and four months after I left her behind in India she departed to heaven.

To that wonderful *Avva*, whose soft touch I still can feel, whose great tales I never can forget, whose sharp intellect I still admire, whose delicious cooking I still can smell, whose funny jokes I still laugh at, whose great wisdom I still cherish and whose God I still worship, to that grandmother I offer my tight embrace. I am sure she received it.

Towards the Hill of Salvation and the Passage of Rebirth

As one gets to the final ascent, which is so also the steepest, it becomes clear that gods are releasing air very sparingly. I paused every few seconds to gasp for

At the Dolma La pass – The Hill of Salvation

breath and my body was sapped of energy. The entire concentration was on counting each step as I struggled to pump some air into my lungs. Gods here seem to deliberately suck oxygen out of the air and simultaneously sanction some to maintain life; a price that one must pay before rebirth. One must drain the body and soul of its old habits and everything is reduced to one breath, one step and one appeal. The air was painfully thin and the mountain looked splendid and incredibly close, and except for three phrases that ran through, my mind was blank. "*Adhbhut!* Splendid is this Form", "Boundless is the Compassion" and "Unfathomable is your Nature". These are the only phrases that passed through my mind. Around here only the present seemed to matter and there was no room for the past and the future. Even the present was reduced to the fundamentals of life – breathing and moving. The ground beneath my feet was unyielding and the air was oppressively thin and as I proceeded the only colourful things were the enticing prayer flags waving along to the wind. Now the goal was in sight and there was something to concentrate on.

Finally, I reached the pass of redemption and salvation presided over by the Goddess Dolma La, the highest point I have ever reached in my life, physically at 18,600 feet and spiritually immeasurable. After passing through deathly grey silence for a considerable period, the colourful prayer flags with their fluttering noises were a welcome sign and relief. Suddenly I felt injected with a strong dose of energy. I trembled with joy, humility and gratitude as I touched the 'Dolma Stone'. I embraced the rock and again for every member of my family. The mountain looked incredibly grand

and overwhelmingly close. My feeling is indescribable for at that high point there were no favours to ask, no pact to be made, no questions to pose and all that one could do was surrender and pay obeisance to its grandeur. A strong wind blew from the mountain towards us sprinkling some powdery snowflakes on us. Nimma appropriately exclaimed, "Showers from Heaven! Gods send their Blessings." Yes, blessings indeed, how else would I be here? BLESSINGS FROM HEAVEN!

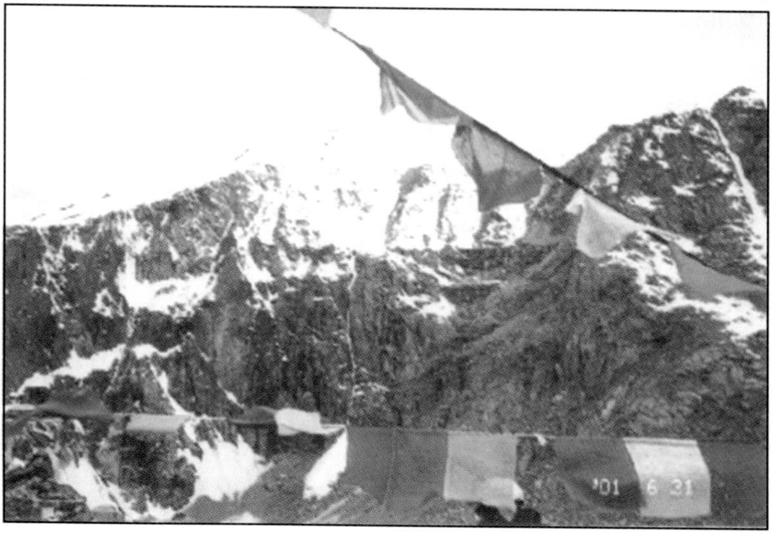
'01 6 31

The Dolma La Pass

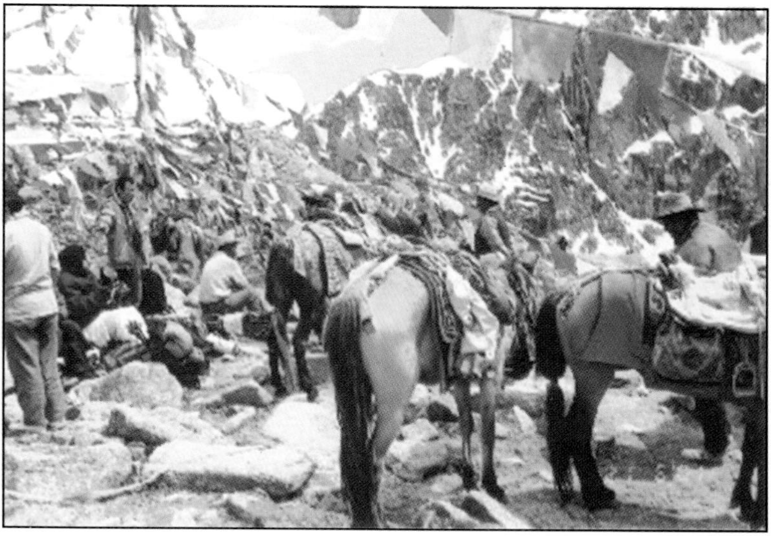

ELEVEN

THE MIRACLE OF DESCENT

As a blade of Kusha *grass can cut the finger when it is wrongly held, asceticism practiced without discrimination can send one on the downward course.*

The Dhammapada *of Buddha, 311*

The summit of consciousness at Dolma La is a place one may be able to reach with a generous supply of Divine aid, but it is not a place to pause and think. It is the high point to be exposed to the lustre of Infinity and absorb whatever radiance the senses possibly can receive. It is a place to experience the power of wordless message and a place to recognise that the Formless Creator is forever busy creating mortal bodies and immortal forms. It is a precious moment when the Mighty Mother holds her child to her bosom and gently slides the newborn on the downward slope. Here, it is The Mother who reigns supreme. The descent has begun and her gravitational pull is strong. She has held her infant upon her knees, tossed her in the air and placed her on a pedestal of a giant nature's slide and now the child must slide carefully monitoring her speed while intelligently using every available scaffold. She is going to watch how her child shall speak to Fate and to the World. More importantly she is going to be watchful to see if her child is sliding smoothly from the heights of consciousness to its depths. Herein lies the challenge of descent.

As a sign of reassurance for the downward journey, the very first encounter as the trail drops is *Gaurikund* – the pond of Gauri. In Tibetan, she is called *Tukje Chenpo Tso* – the Lake of Great Mercy. At 18,400 feet it is perhaps one of the highest lakes in the world. This small frigid green lake amidst icy cliffs is said to remain frozen all year long. There is a romantic aura to this lake, for it is here that love blossomed between Parvati and Shiva. Scriptures note that Parvati did penance around here to win Shiva's heart and it is in this lake that she bathed before marrying Shiva. The yellow and red coloured mineral deposits on the rocks resembling sprinkled turmeric and vermilion add to the auspicious flair.

Having reached the Dolma La Pass, I thought all the trials and tribulations were over. My body and mind were totally unprepared for the challenges of descent and so the real trial began. I must descend a very steep trail, carefully treading on huge boulders of every shape and size. Some rocks were hanging rather precariously on other rocks. Having sanctioned a new life, Gods now put you to test to see what you make of it. Contrary to the ascent where I felt I was shedding some weight, every step in the descent felt burdensome, as if I was carrying five hundred pounds on my back. The terrain was made up of angular blocks of rock stacked atop one another rather irregularly. A slight movement in any one of the rocks can have a devastating domino effect. During the ascent Gods seem to lend their helping hand and participate in your struggle, now they seem to be cheering spectators. Their hands-off approach is perhaps to show the pilgrim the miracle of descent. The more I think about the difficulty of descent, I realise that my body's struggle is only an emblem of a complex theorem in spiritual pursuit.

The path of spiritual realisation can be classified broadly into two philosophical systems – one the path of distinction and discrimination and the other the path of union and integration. The former is the *Viveka Marga*—the intellectual path that requires the mind to be released from the trappings of limited body and matter. The spiritual path is a linear trajectory and consciousness ascends and eventually transcends. The school of Vedanta belongs in this category and in particular the works of *Adi Sankaracharya* epitomises this philosophy. In his classic works like *Atma Bodha*—'Self Knowledge' and *Viveka Chudamani* – 'Crest Jewel of Discrimination', Sankaracharya asserts that the only way to liberate ourselves is to rise from the illusory world. Thus, in this formula *Samsara* – the phenomenal world— is false and illusory while Brahman, the Cosmic Self is the Truth. The *Yoga Sutras* of Patanjali also fall into this category, as Yoga to him is an intense state of abstract meditation called *Samadhi*. According to this school of thought spiritual realisation is a linear irreversible path.

The other approach to spiritual realisation is the *Yogaja Marga* – the path of union and integration. The ideal here is not the rejection of the world as illusory, but its assimilation into its Supra Cosmic source, after delineating the distinctions between the concrete and abstract, individual self and Cosmic Self. Therefore the movement in this path is curvilinear in which the ascent must be followed by a 'redescent' to complete spiritual journey. Each half of the journey has its unique characteristics and unique challenges, and neither one is superior to the other. The school of Kashmir Saivism and Abhinavagupta's exposition of Tantric philosophy and the Integral Yoga proposed by Sri Aurobindo belong to this category. This school does not negate the principles of ascent and abstraction, but adds the necessary principles of descent to the concrete matter, making it holistic.

Abhinavagupta, belonging to the school of Kashmir Saivism was a great theoretician of aesthetics and dramatic art forms, and therefore in his philosophies the earthly and the ethereal blend. As a totalising philosopher, his system synthesises within single framework entire realm of experiences like Tantric ritual, everyday worldly transactions, aesthetics of theatre and transgressive practices. To him the highest form of spiritual realisation is the all-devouring Bhairava Consciousness, which has two successive modes. The first one is called *Sankoca*—'the ascending mode' in which the activity is contraction, which is isolating itself from body, world etc., to a higher level of pure abstraction. Therefore the entire concentration is on renunciation, ritual purity, yogic asceticism and withdrawal. But the spiritual journey is complete only when the consciousness begins to expand and assimilate the lower forms of impure concrete matter and transforming them, thereby universalising all aspects of existence. In this integration process all boundaries between Higher and Lower, pure and impure, individual self and Cosmic Self are erased. Unlike the world negating Vedantic philosophy, the *Saivagama* philosophy is world embracing. The embrace is not in an undifferentiated state, but after considerable differentiation during the ascent, it redescends with a heightened consciousness to absorb the world. The images and metaphors used in the intellectual path are separation, dispassion and focused concentration, whereas the integral path utilises images of vastness, extensive space and merger with the Cosmic Reality to break down all barriers. The text of Kashmir Saivism *Vijnanabhairava or* 'Divine Consciousness' very freely uses sensuous experiences and sexual metaphors to depict the union between the self and the Divine.

Like Abhinavagupta, Sri Aurobindo also has given the most profound exposition of Integral Yoga, which does not dismiss the world as illusory. The practice of Integral Yoga is bi-directional—the first one is the ascent of human consciousness to the higher plane and this is followed by the descent of divine power to earth consciousness. It is the descent that can eliminate darkness and ignorance and transform the world. Sri Aurobindo recognising this fact, asserts that Brahman resides both in the human world and in the Supra Cosmic world. To recognise it in the prosaic world of daily life is a greater challenge. To absorb divine light and power one must constantly widen the consciousness. Failure to do so prevents us from recognising godliness in the earthly life.

Sri Aurobindo points out the descent of divine light into lower being, into daily life and the body is an absolute necessity for the transformation of individual consciousness. If higher consciousness remains at the heights and the lower remains at the lower realms the heightened consciousness remains detached and becomes useless. Therefore the individual consciousness must actively toss the lid and allow the influx of Spirit to percolate through the cellular level and allow metamorphosis. Only then the luminosity of higher truth and wisdom is capable of dispelling darkness and a fundamental change in the Being, and in the world is possible. Sri Aurobindo clearly cautions that there are greater difficulties in the descent. In the process of ascent one readily sheds old habits in search of something superior, but during the descent the individual shows resistance and closes all loopholes for the Power to sink in. To bring profoundness into the vagaries of life is confusing, unsettling and laborious and herein lies the challenge of descent.

The idea of descent and totalising consciousness is most forcefully asserted in Western philosophy by Nietzsche, who argued that 'eternal recurrence' is needed for the 'will to power'. Nietzsche argues that both the 'mechanistic and Platonic' – the mundane and the idealistic are reconciled in the eternal recurrence. Without the eternal recurrence he said that 'eternal novelty' capable of transforming the 'finite', and the 'definite' is not possible. The principle of eternal recurrence alone can maintain the power of infinite novelty, allowing new modes of interpretation, device new analytical categories and re-evaluate old formulae. He said in his famous work *Will to Power*, "The world, even if it is no longer a god, is still supposed to be capable of the divine power of creation, the power of infinite transformations; it is supposed to consciously prevent itself from returning to any of its old forms; it is supposed to possess not only the intention but the *means* of avoiding any repetition; to that end it is supposed to control every one of its

Gaurikund – 'the pond of Gauri'
Parvati bathed here before marrying Shiva.

movements at every moment so as to escape goals, final states, repetitions – whatever else may follow from such an unforgivably insane way of thinking and desiring." [*Will to Power* 1062 (1885)] Neitzsche in his familiar vitriolic tone says that failure of ideas and ideals to touch life constitutes an Egyptian 'Mummifed Consciousness", that has its own existence contributing to the tragedy in philosophy.*

During the descent my body and mind experienced unknown dangers, unknown challenges and unknown fears about where my next step would take me. Will my feet land on a firm rock or would I go tumbling down? Will I be able to connect spirituality to daily life or would it remain to be a phantom idea? If I bring abstract ideas and ideals to life, would I be able to choose the right context, right time, or would I connect it to a loose boulder of life event and let it all crumble? Should I choose to step on safer and smoother rocks and risk losing my way or stay on the rough path to reach my destination? Can one be an escapist and evade these tough challenges or should one thoughtfully apply what has been experienced at heights to creatively meet the challenge? Every downward movement seemed to be filled with risks and fears and about the appropriateness of the move and of the link and this is a heavy burden. The burden is not because Gods have applied pressure from above, but because I resisted their entry into me. It is easier to leave God in the temple and conduct my business as usual, but to assimilate

---

* See Friedrich Nietzsche, *The Will to Power*. Translated by Walter Kaufman and R.J. Hollingdale. Vintage Books. New York.
* Also see Friedrich Nietzsche, *Twilight of the Idols/The Anti-Christ*. Translated by R.J. Hollingdale.

the power and allow the quiet flow needs some practice and a lot of miracles.

Despite all the challenges of descending over huge rocks and crossing icy glaciers, at least my body managed to reach the plains without tumbling down or slipping. Clearly there was a generous supply of miracles. About spiritual descent and transformation only future can tell and it is a life long task. I am sure in that realm there are bound to be many slips and falls.

Before reaching the pastoral green valley, as a reminder that invisible forces assist you in all the trials, you see a huge rock in the shape of an axe. Nimma told me that it is the 'Axe of Karma' – all your karmic misdeeds of the past are axed and nullified by the mercy of the benevolent mother Dolma.

The eastern valley is the land of miracles, for in this region is the famous Dzundulphug cave where Tibet's poet – saint Milarepa performed miracles and reached the top of Kailash. In his famous work *One Hundred Thousand Songs*, Milarepa has recorded "The Miracle Contest on Di Se Snow Mountain" with a Bon priest Nara Bhun Chon. The Bon priest humiliates Milarepa and dismisses him as shallow and insignificant in thought and deed and challenges him to demonstrate his miraculous power. Milarepa in response seated himself above Lake Manasarovar and appeared to cover the whole lake without making his body larger and the lake smaller. To further convince the Bon priest, Milarepa performed another miracle by putting the whole lake on his fingertip. The magician then invites Milarepa into a race to climb to the summit of Mount Kailash. Before sunrise the Bon priest appeared to be close to the summit while Milarepa rested for a while waiting for the first rays of sun to appear. The Bon priest mocks at Milarepa, being convinced that he would win the race, but exactly at the same moment when the first ray of sun touched the holy mountain, Milarepa appeared on top of Kailash and thus proclaimed in his poetry:

> On the Mountain, the Snow Di Se,
> I, the Yogi of Tibet, with the Dharma Conquer Bon,
> And make the Buddha Practice Lineage illuminate Tibet.
> This is my strength, the strength of Milarepa.
> With it I have now conquered heretics,
> Hereafter I shall be master of Di Se Snow Mountain,
> Whence I shall propagate the Buddha's teachings
> To you, oh Wisdom-Deities, I give worship and pray.
>
> *The Hundred Thousand*
> *Songs of Milarepa*. Volume I

According to the legend, Milarepa sang and meditated in the cave of Dzundulphug in the eastern valley, and the pilgrim is shown the imprint of his hand on the ceiling of the cave and his footprint on top of the cave as a proof. As the story goes Milarepa found the cave too low and hence pushed the ceiling with his bare hand, but his force was too strong and the cave got too high for comfort, and so he pressed it down with one foot until it came to a desirable level. Milarepa's songs were kept alive by his faithful descendents and his immediate disciple and biographer was Rechung. Even to this day Milarepa's songs are sung all over Tibet.

From the eastern valley, Kailash is not at all visible, but it has its own charm and comfort level. The soft green grass on the ground contrasting the colourful mineral deposits on the rocks provides a fairytale ambience for the newborn. The third day of the *Kora* was colourful and reassuring. The new life seemed promising as the Gods seemed to have painted the region with soothing colours to receive the exhausted child coming down a giant slide. The ground felt well padded with green grass for a soft landing. During the last stretch of *Kora* it felt good to lie down on this soft bed and gaze into the blue sky once in a while just to feel the body merge into the grass and the space. The sensory experience from the tactile to the visual to the auditory was like a gentle massage to the overworked body.

In the last leg of the *Kora*, Lake Rakhshas Tal comes into view, as if like a reminder that dark forces are continually generated in the Lake of the Moon. From a distance this streak of intense turquoise looked splendid and inviting. Base energy is always very tempting. But things around me were far too pleasant for me to dig into my subconscious reservoir. I know it will hover over me very soon, whether I like it or not. But this moment was reserved for exuberance and vitality.

I was not anticipating the finish line; the narrow path gently curved and I saw our drivers cheering and all of them shouted in a chorus, "*Om Namah Sivaya*", and even before I could join the chorus, I turned around prostrated towards the mountain and sobbed once again uncontrollably. I could not contain my joyous tears, I prostrated again and again and nothing I did could express my gratitude.

Words cannot express the sensations I felt at that moment. It is indeed grace at its best that even a small insignificant being like me is incorporated into the cosmic orbit. All creation revolves around Meru; it is

Crossing icy glaciers during the descent

The challenge of descent

the centre of the circle of God, the navel of the universe, the centre of the creative energy, and to circle its physical manifestation is like being part of the whole. From every vantage point in the circuit, grace is showered from the founts of the Eternal and Supreme. This Creator of things in his all-knowing sleep and all-pervading dance sets everything in motion. Locked in his orbit and captured in his gaze one cannot lose the way. In this inner circle gifts are plentiful; one must only be prepared to receive them. I don't know how much nectar I spilled from my porous trembling hands, nor do I know how many secret whispers from the rocks that my deaf ears failed to register, but I do know that many of my conscious desires were brought to fruition in this circuit. A daughter's search for her Father, a devotee's longing for a Personal God, a weary traveller's need for a Guide, a singer's penance for Sound, a pilgrim's quest for Shrine have been answered without any trace of doubt.

When the Great Dancer takes his spontaneous steps, the path is paved for his children and along the way when he extends his helping hand one is dancing with the Gods. So precious is this union and so joyous are the movements with the Cosmic Dancer and so lovely is the memory locked in the feet. The earth that I kissed in gratitude felt like perfect heaven, and this is the miracle of descent. When you know that the Great Dancer is your dancing partner, it is the miracle of descent. When you are no longer in search of a ladder to the heaven, it is the miracle of descent. When you can laugh and mock at the demigods and affirm that God is also on your side, it is the miracle of descent. When you can roam in this part of the world without any injury, it is the miracle of descent. When you feel you are part of the Celestial Choral Dance, it is the miracle of descent. When I finally sing the song of my heart to you all, it is also a *miracle of descent*. To these magical moments of union supported by so many invisible forces, I sang Mangalam – hymn of salutation to mark the occasion.

Felicitations to the *Om*, Felicitations to the *Omkara* Felicitations to that preceptor *Om Namah Sivaya*.

Felicitations to the sound *Na*, Felicitations to the syllable *Na*. Felicitations to that preceptor worshipped by Nama Deva.

Felicitations to the sound *Ma*, Felicitations to the syllable *Ma* Felicitations to that ONE worshipped by all the Great Gods.

Felicitations to the sound *Si*, Felicitations to the syllable *Si* Felicitations to that ONE worshipped by Siddhi and Buddhi.

Felicitations to the sound *Va*, Felicitations to the syllable *Va* Felicitations to that ONE worshipped by Vama Deva.

Felicitations to the sound *Ya*, Felicitations to the syllable *Ya* Felicitations to HIM worshipped by Yagna Rupa.

Prayer of gratitude after completing the Parikrama

TWELVE

MANASAROVAR: THE FECUND LAKE OF THE MIND

✣

*Whoever touches his body with earth from Manasarovar and
bathes in its waters will attain to the paradise of Brahma,
and whoever drinks the water will ascend to the heaven of
Siva and be washed pure from the sins of hundred incarnations,
and even animals which bear the name Manasarovar will
enter into Brahma's paradise. Its waters are like pearls.*
Manasa Khanda

Long before Creation happened, the whole universe
was submerged in the Primordial Ocean and the only
one floating on this ocean was Lord Vishnu in deep
meditation. However, his consciousness was wide-
awake and he saw countless worlds merged in his own
body. By the force of Time, the creative powers within
him surged, and a lotus with Brahma seated on top of
it came out of the navel of Lord Vishnu. Thus, the
Divine Creative Power is concentrated within Brahma.
From the uproarious waves of the ocean, the thickened
land emerged and a mountain rose at the navel of this
newborn earth. Kailash is the embodiment of that
mythical mountain Sumeru. When the first sons of
Brahma who were learned sages came to the Kailash

region for meditation and worship, they needed sanctified water to bathe and conduct other rituals. They appealed to their father, and Brahma created Manasarovar from the will power of his mind. Born out of Brahma's mind, this lake is an emblem of beauty, intellect, purity and enlightened knowledge. Mount Kailash and Lake Manasarovar complement each other in every aspect – the height to its depth, the spirit to its matter, the erotic to the sublime and the immutable to the mutable. If Kailash is the Absolute Centre of Divinity, a much-adored shrine, Manasarovar is the fluid form that delivers one to the realm of the Absolute.

Geographically, the significance of Manasarovar cannot be understated. At an altitude of 15,000 feet it is the highest fresh water lake in the world. More importantly, this lake is the mother of four majestic rivers – Indus, Brahmaputra, Sutlej and Karnali that flow in four different directions. Tibetans call this *Tso Mapham* 'The Undefeated Lake' or *Tso Rinpoche* 'The Precious Lake'. The rivers that flow out of this lake are long and they make vast regions of the Indian sub-continent fertile. Manasarovar's significance goes beyond the physical aspects of the lake. It is a profound symbol of everything that humanity must aspire for. It is the mind's lake symbolising creative energy that human beings must engage in to make the mind more fertile. Taking a dip in that lake is to absorb the creative powers of Brahma.

The Sanskrit word *'Manas'* is derived from *'Man'* meaning "intellect, intelligence, understanding, perception, sense, conscience, will" (Monier-Williams, *A Sanskrit Dictionary*, p.783), and it refers to all mental powers having strong emotional connotations. The round shaped Manasarovar resembling the sun signifies solar energy capable of expelling darkness due to ignorance. A dip in the lake is said to cleanse the mind of impure and inert ideas and generate sublime and lofty patterns of thought that are creative and useful in the spiritual ascent.

The merits of the dip cannot be taken all too literally. It is a symbolic prelude or an intermediary step in the process of spiritual growth. It is an effective demonstrative lesson on methods of achieving clarity of the mind. The lake is both the goal and the method for spiritual contemplation. This symbolic act when internalised with utmost seriousness and sincerity shows you the way to rid the mind of unchaste ideas and creates a potential for some higher thought processes to emerge. The Lake is simultaneously a cleanser of the tarnished mind and a generator of new ideas and ideals when approached with the right intent. The secret lies in the partnership between the Lake and the individual. The Lake is the repository of profound knowledge and wisdom of the Creative Divinity and a dip in it is a unique opportunity for the pilgrims to absorb whatever little they can. It is meant to quench the thirsty mind.

If Brahma's lake is an idea, a concept and a metaphor, where then do we find its quintessential manifestation? The great poet Goswami Tulsidas presents us with the finest expression of the holy Lake in his poetic rendition of Rama's tale – "*Ram Charit Manas*". For Tulsidas the 'holy lake of the mind' is undoubtedly the 'living legend of Rama' and the contemplative mind, like the mythical *Hamsa* (swan) floats on these pure waters and feeds on the pearls plucked from the lake's clear waters. In Tulsi's allegorical framework, the mystical lake exists on the 'soil of good intelligence' that draws its sweetness by distilling water from the boundless ocean of scriptures and Vedas. Like the swan that is capable of separating milk from water, Tulsidas states that the learned sages have extracted the sweet essence of Rama's tales from the vast ocean of scriptures, and as clouds they have showered the earth with sweet water. Tulsidas writes that the ambrosial rainwater collected in the lake is the glory of Rama and Sita and his similes are the beckoning wavelets of the lake and his stanzas are the 'beautiful lotus beds' and the 'elegance of expression' is the 'mother-of-pearl'. Tulsidas invites his readers to immerse themselves in this holy lake of Rama's deeds and collect its pure waters and let it flow into the 'lake of the soul', so that earthly life is made beautiful and refreshing. (*Bal Khand*)

Tulsidas credits Lord Shiva himself for presenting him with the image of 'Manas Lake' to narrate the story of Rama. Like the heights of Kailash, the depth of Manasarovar is also immeasurable and unfathomable. From the mountain heights Shiva is said to have contemplated about the significance of this heavenly lake for the welfare of human beings and after years of intense meditation pronounced that Rama's tale is the lake in which seeking souls must take a dip and drink its waters, as Tulsidas states early on in his narrative:

> "Having conceived it Shiva treasured it in his mind till at an auspicious moment he declared it to Uma; thus Shiva looking into his own soul and rejoicing it gave it the excellent name of Ram Charit Manas. And this is the blessed legend that I repeat; hear it good people, reverently and attentively". (*Bal Khand*)

Taking the image of *Manas Lake* as a blessing from Lord Shiva, Tulsidas goes on to describe every dimension of the 'Holy Lake of Rama's deeds'. He describes the four ghats of the lake as 'four charming dialogues contrived by divine wisdom' and the seven cantos of the epic narrative as seven 'flights of steps' taking the soul into the 'clear and deep expanse' of the unsullied greatness of Sri Rama.

Tulsidas's metaphor leaves one wondering whether it is his narrative pull that enhances the beauty of Manasarovar or is it the splendor of raw nature from which these metaphors are derived that support the narrative. Perhaps the configuration of words and the configuration of nature create and support each other. Whatever the interface between the 'word' and the 'nature' might be, one truth is upheld. Manasarovar being the 'Primeval Lake' is the mother of all rivers in this region and Ramayan being the '*Adi Kavya*' – the first poem is the mother of all poetic genres in this multi-lingual region of South Asia and both nourish the soul.

The lake that our senses perceive is quite different from the lake of poetic imagination. Scriptures and other texts describe Manasarovar as Brahma's Paradise, where the '*Raja Hamsa*' – the royal swans, the emblem of Brahma glide on its transparent waters and lotus beds cover vast portions of the Lake. It is said to be surrounded by lush green trees and perched on the branches are songbirds warbling out melodious tunes and the cool mountain breeze carries the pleasant fragrance of seasonal flowers. In reality, there are no swans and lotus beds floating on the Lake and there are no green trees or plants with fragrant flowers surrounding the Lake. In this desolate highland, the moving clouds lit by fierce sunshine forming a rich tapestry of colors were the only ornaments suspended in between the intense blue sky and the turquoise blue lake. Stripped of all other accessories, the lake seems to bare its soul in all its naked beauty against the backdrop of raw nature and that was dazzling enough. Having circled the immutable form of the Divine, I was more than eager to plunge into its fluid form.

As I walked towards the lake from the camping site, it seemed to play tricks on my senses; the longer I walked, the farther the lake seemed to be receding from me. Finally the grass and gravel surface below my feet yielded to the sand dunes and I stood at the shores of Manasarovar. I gazed over the 'infinity of blue'; the lake stretched as far as the eyes can see and beyond. The lake stretches 15 miles in width and 55 miles in circumference and my lens was incapable of covering the range. My attention was riveted towards things near and immediate: the gentle waves rose to some celestial rhythm and their movements were as graceful as the 'swan dance'. On that late afternoon *Surya Dev* or the Sun God seemed to have sprinkled the blue waters with sparkling gems. The wavelets brought soothing musical sounds along with other gifts from gods like smoothly rounded pebbles and seaweed that have healing properties as they reached the shore. I was simply amazed to see the exchange at the shoreline; the waves brought smooth pebbles from the depths of the lake and simultaneously sucked the rough gravel on the shores. The message was crystal clear; enter the lake with all your rough edges and come out in fine fettle. This is the Creative Power of the Divine. The lake was sparkling and the surrounding sand dunes merrily glistened. Undoubtedly this is Brahma's Paradise.

Gazing at the magnificent lake, I knelt on the shingled beach and collected the holy water in my cupped hands, and drank it with a deep sense of gratitude and reverence. It is said that the Cosmic Soul is multi-visaged and just the touch of this fluid form can alter the fixed plan of Fate. I do not know what adjustments were made in my fate's or destiny's plan, but I do know that the sensation of water trickling over and within my body felt like my soul's communion with the Infinite. I scooped the waters several times in my cupped hands with a mixture of awe, eagerness and hesitation, hesitance because I wondered about my worthiness for this unique experience. But the thrill of splashing and drinking the holy waters was far too overpowering that these self-doubts were quickly suppressed. The moment was far too magical for doubts to rise. I felt so *awakened* and *alive* by the touch of unseen forces and without wasting any more time at the shore I waded through the shallow waters to go farther into the lake.

It was playtime and all the celestial bodies offered their co-operation. The sun was shining brilliantly and became a natural geyser to heat the lake waters to a tolerable level. As the gentle waves lapped at my knees, I saw Mount Kailash at a clear distance. How often does one get a chance to see one form of the Divine while immersed in another form? This is a blessed moment. I do not know what chance encounters are in store for me in future and what rearrangements have been made in my fate's plan and how many misdeeds are being washed away. But I do know that these magical moments will stay with me forever guiding me to reinterpret chance and fate. Sri Aurobindo's words emphasise the need to reinterpret and reevaluate meanings in his classic work *Savitri*:

> The Cosmos is no accident in Time;
> There is a meaning in each play of Chance,
> There is a freedom in each face of Fate.
> (Book II, Canto 11, p.308)

This moment was reserved for play in this heavenly lake, and so I waded through the waters, plunged, rolled over and soaked myself in the waters. Facing Mount Kailash I chanted appropriately the *Shiva Manasa Stotra* 'Hymn in praise of Shiva of the Mind'. My mind's eye saw the heavenly priests performing the ritual ablution of the Divine Idol, while I was seeking my own absolution by ablution in the lake. It felt like being in one grand congregation receiving wordless messages amplified by the winds from the high white pulpit of the Gods. The God's kingdom looks grand and sounds perfect and the sensation of never ending waves tapping on my body was so soothing and the lake's sweet water quenched my thirst. I remembered that there were many thirsting family members and friends' back home and so duly collected the lake water in the bottles.

These waters are infused with so many great legends, myths and poetic beauty, that to sip even one drop amounts to absorbing grace, spirit and life. Milarepa describes this lake as a 'green-gemmed Mandala' and as the 'fountainhead of four great rivers'. Taken as a metaphor the streams flowing in four directions are meant to cool the scorched soul, and its ambrosial nectar is the remedy for the ailing life. Milarepa explains the reason:

> Because it is the Eight Nagas' dwelling,
> It appears to be a Mandala made of gems,
> The water falling in it from the heavens

Entry into Lake Manasarovar

Playful at Lake Manasarovar

Dip in Lake Manasarovar

Prayers in Lake Manasarovar

Is like a stream of milk, a rain of nectar;
It is the Hundred Devas' bathing place,
The water with eight merits.

One Hundred Thousand Songs of Milarepa

The legend of The Buddha says that Queen Maya bathed in this lake to rid her body of all the impurities before The Buddha appearing like the white elephant in the cloud, from the direction of Mount Kailash entered her womb. Together, the Mountain and the Lake symbolise the 'Pure White Buddhist Doctrine'. As my wet shivering body struggled to bottle the water, I wondered about the effort needed to bottle the Doctrine. A greater challenge is to be able to consume and digest the Doctrine. But for now, the water seems to be a good beginning.

As dusk fell, colours wove their magic around the entire circuit. Mother Nature in all her glory was adorned with too many uncut precious stones like rubies, diamonds, pearls, opal, amethyst, lapis lazuli and aquamarine; and this crowning ornamentation made her look so regal and resplendent. The coronation ceremony amidst the colourful pageantry had to come to an end as darkness fell and the waters were turning icy cold. It was time to return to the tent.

By the crack of dawn, I hurriedly walked to the lake to absorb the spiritual vibrations at that significant hour, before bidding farewell. The lake's temperament was quite different from the previous evening. Stillness prevailed and it looked as if the lake stretched immobile on a mat of silence. There were no dancing wavelets or sparkling gems on its surface. This is not playtime. It is time to concentrate on the deep meditative stillness of the lake and attune your inner self to that calmness. A wavering mind will never be able to gain awareness of all the hidden treasures in the mind's lake.

It is recorded in *Siva Purana* that the earth is made up of seven *Dvipas* (continents) – Jambu, Plaksa, Salmali, Kusa, Kraunca, Saka and Puskara and they are surrounded by seven oceans. Jambu Dvipa is in the middle of all these and from its navel rises the Meru Parvat as the mythical version of Mount Kailash. At its feet is the Lake Manasarovar and in the centre of this lake grows *Jambu Tree* – 'The Tree of Knowledge' or 'The Tree of Life' as a flagstaff of this sacred shrine. The seeker of knowledge consumes the fruit of this tree and wears its seed called *Jambunada* as an ornament. (*Uma Samhita*, Chapter 17)

This tree is invisible to the mortal eyes. It requires intense *sadhana* – spiritual practice for many years, over many births even to recognise the treasures and perhaps many more to extract the juice from its fruit. But, the lake is generous and clear in its lesson plan. Even a simpleton pilgrim receives a valuable lesson. When I looked at my image in this grand liquid mirror on the roof of the world, the lesson was clear – *"Look Within Yourself"*. The treasures contained in the depths of Manasarovar are reflected in the depths of your consciousness. The lesson repeated itself while I sat on the shores of the lake in sublime joy gazing at the vast expanse of space. When I closed my eyes to capture the image of a personal god, the same instructions continued. The more I heard it in this heavenly classroom, the more compelling was the message. In the Silence that prevailed in the air, the wordless message was crystal clear and I wanted to hear more as a perfect encore to a celestial concert.

The still waters of Manasarovar at dawn

As I bid farewell to this magnificent shrine, I hoped that these instructions would ring into my ears in the post-pilgrimage life. I wished that the image captured in my mind's eye would re-present itself when I struggle to plumb the depths of my consciousness. The mind, like the lake must have infinite regenerative capacity for dissolution and recreation of thoughts. The water particles from the lake evaporate and rise to form clouds only to rain on the earth as purer water. Likewise, the mind must have the strength and the will power to reflect, re-evaluate and re-interpret old and established fixed thoughts and refurbish it with novel thoughts that respond appropriately to historical time and cultural space. Like Manasarovar, the mind must always be a symbol of fecundity.

THIRTEEN

RETURN OF THE PILGRIM

✝

"What language is thine, O Sea?"
"The language of eternal question."
"What language is thy answer, O Sky?"
"The language of eternal silence." (12)

God's silence ripens man's thoughts into speech. (304)

Thou wilt find, Eternal Traveller, marks of thy footsteps across my songs. (305)

Rabindranath Tagore, *Stray Birds*.

How can Eternal Silence be a satisfactory response to eternal questions? Until one experiences this extraordinary exchange, it is not possible to believe in the power of wordless messages. There is nothing more gratifying than a good dialogue – to hear and to be heard, and so wonderful is this feeling for faith. On this grand roof of the world, so unwavering and confident is the Silence and despite its exalted status it responds to the humble but noisy prose of life's questions. Perhaps, these are sentimental feelings of a foolish pilgrim, but then who cares? I take Nietzsche's Zarathustra's advice more seriously, "better to be foolish with happiness than foolish with misfortune, better to dance clumsily than to walk lamely." After all, I came here seeking a dance of the soul and despite my clumsy movements, it was difficult to leave the dance floor on this elevated stage. The show had to come to an abrupt end, as the Sherpas were anxious to cross the Chinese border in three days. As I bid final farewell, I made my wish quite clear: a wish that the marks of the Cosmic Dancer's footsteps will surface in my songs, in my life and in my world.

The return journey had a great sense of practical urgency: we had to cross the border before the visa and the road permit expired. The Sherpas were in no mood for Chinese bureaucracy and we pilgrims were eager to catch our respective flights. After our initial borderland troubles, we had forgotten all about the Chinese; it was as if they never entered Tibet. Immersed in the glory of Kailash-Manasarovar, everything about Chinese checkpoints and official formalities faded from our memory, and thankfully along with that, earlier restlessness and anxiety also left my system. I have seen Kailash and Manasarovar and what can the Chinese do now? Except for bidding sad farewell to our skillful and cheerful Tibetan drivers and guide, exiting China was uneventful. It is only at the border crossing that I became forcibly aware of the Chinese presence, whereas in the interiors I knew I was on the Tibetan soil, although the demolished monasteries were grim reminders of Chinese heavy handedness. When I set foot on the Friendship Bridge, I felt sorry to leave Tibet, but relieved to leave China. It was an inevitable dual response to invasion and on-going oppression and exploitation.

The final stretch of our journey from the Tibet–Nepal border to our hotel in Kathmandu was filled with all sorts of adventures, narrow escapes and delays. We escaped several landslides and at one point waded through sticky mudslides to switch buses; and at another point stranded for long hours waiting for the emergency crew to clear the debris. In addition to all this, we survived the feats of our reckless driver at the steering wheel. The Power of Kailash protected all of us and I knew my mother's prayers contributed to my safe return. From the hotel lobby I called my mother and the joy and relief in her voice brought Kailash pilgrimage to a meaningful conclusion.

A day after I arrived in New Delhi, I set out on yet another Himalayan adventure in the exotic Garhwal region. I was held captive to the Himalayan mystique and was eager to see another face of the mountain range from the Indian side. The majestic mountain range kept its promise to show another facet and gave a different experience. Unlike the vast expanse of space on the Tibetan plateau that mystified me, the lush greenery of the mountains with winding rivers sliding through them from great heights charmed me. I trekked to the heights of *Yamunotri* – an arbitrary birthplace of river Yamuna. Her path is enticing and beautiful; so bewitching is her body that even Lord Krishna could not resist her charm. She is playful and reassuring and beckons you to bathe in her waters without any fears. The feeling was different when I trekked to *Gangotri* – the birthplace of the mighty Ganges. All along her path she shows her power and ferocity. The force with which she drops from the mountains is terrifying and you have no choice but to fold your hands and bow to her might. There is nothing playful about Ganga: she is the ticket to salvation. Her currents are strong, despite the fact that Lord Shiva arrested her in his matted hair while she was descending from the heavens and then gently released the knot to tame her irrepressible nature.

Each day in the Himalayan journey brought new sensations and feelings never experienced before. The slopes and the valleys are filled with plants that have medicinal properties and their pleasant fragrance gives natural aroma therapy. Inexhaustible is the Himalayan wonder and tucked in these mountains are innumerable shrines with their own fascinating legends. It is impossible to walk out of the Himalayan terrain voluntarily, but your other obligations and commitments force you to record these experiences in your memory storehouse only to be replayed whenever the heart longs for it.

Like the carefree bird that willingly flies into exotic regions rejoices equally in returning to the safety and familiarity of its nest, I happily arrived in New York City on August 5, 2001. I had no idea that while I was spinning adventure tales about gods, mountains and lakes to anybody with inquisitive ears, there were men hiding in the mountain caves of Afghanistan devising a plot so diabolic that I would actually witness the horror straight from my window. I woke up on September 11 2001, eager to start the new academic year and along with my routine lesson plans, I was busy fusing myths and mountains to construct a story for my friends and students only to be interrupted by a news alert on my computer screen. A plane crashed into the north tower of the World Trade Center, I turned on the TV and saw another plane crashing into the south tower. Thus began the horror story for our collective humanity.

Experiences gain significance within certain cultural contexts and become relevant at certain historical times and are interesting only to a select group of listeners. Above all, past experiences can be drawn into conscious thought processes only when the mood is right. All narratives must obey the laws of time and space, capable of mediating the exchange between the speaker and the listener, and for that matter even within the thinker. In the immediate post 9/11 life, it was impossible to remind myself of the grandeur of Himalayas and the tranquility it offers. To dwell in that world seemed either timid denial or cruel indifference to pain and suffering. How can one think of vast expanse of space, clean air and mighty mountains, while the rescuers working in congested areas breathing toxic air were pulling out commingled body parts lying under a mountain of metallic debris?

The terrorist attack of September 11 generated a host of discussions and debates on Islamic *Jihad*, psychology of suicide bombers, fundamentalism, religious intolerance and secular ideologies and axiomatically some version of 'God' was inserted into these discourses. While the victims of terrorism, direct or indirect, with their own diverse pasts and belief systems – faith based or otherwise—were struggling to develop their sense of tolerance and mutual co-existence in pluralistic societies, the religious and political leaders have been cleverly exploiting this tension and fear. The religious and political leaders have been busy manufacturing packaged forms of ancient faiths with ready-made theories of violence and hatred to the vulnerable and unsuspecting masses. The packaging is done with some uncanny authenticity by choosing

passages from scriptures taken out of their context to
suit their political agenda. In this unsettling climate the
poetics of my very private pilgrimage came face to face
with the politics of religion.

The Himalayan experience revealed the purity of
Silence – a very godly silence in the grandeur of Nature,
and its deep valleys and precipices indicated the depths
to which the consciousness must probe in order to leap
to the heights to commune with the Universal Being.
The 'Silence of God' that was so invigorating entered
into dialectic with the frustrating loud talk about god
and civilizations in the wake of the September 11
terrorist attack. I was not struggling with my 'personal
feeling for the Divine Being', nor was I entering into a
debate between 'my God' versus 'other Gods'. It was
really between 'individual faith' – practised as a way
of life by people of every religious denomination
making their belief systems operationally plural and
tolerant and 'religious ideology' with vested political
interests prescribed in various corners of the society.

The individual practice and the abstract codes of the
belief system although not mutually exclusive seem to
have different concerns, demands and outcomes. The
former inevitably makes room for cultural variation and
historical specificity because human consciousness is
heterogeneous and changes with time. Drawing from
scriptures and other sources individuals make their
private god who could respond to their personal
concerns. In this system local deities emerge celebrating
local customs and rituals. This kind of living faith
facilitates personal expression and meaning and
celebrates collective carnival that is colourful and
liberating. There are no hierarchies in this system;

everything co-exists on a lateral plane. Religion as an ideology on the other hand, particularly the mass production type that we are bombarded with lately from every corner and from every religious brand, strictly enforces uniformity in their codes inviting not creative interpretation but literal reading of the text. It dishonours the specifics of culture and history and demands absolute allegiance. Like a commodity in the market economy, the ideology is packaged attractively and advertised as 'superior' to other brands. While the personal faith creates possibilities for Self-Realisation, religious ideology forces self-affirmation along with a ruthless negation of the other. With Self-Realisation there is some scope to recognise that the same love one has towards their 'god' is what others have towards their gods. Personal faith seems like a spectator within us that finds meaning in the world drama from the unity of performers playing different roles; but ideology lures you into the battlefield and arms you with religious icons and slogans taken out of context to create a mass frenzy. Faith grows with life, finds unity in diversity and rejoices in the variety created by some higher power, whereas ideology forcefully thrusts fixed and ready-made doctrines demanding loyalty in the battleground. When faith slips into ideology everything enters into a Darwinian race.

The spiritual aspirant seeks liberation from the shackles of daily life in search of salvation; but how does this concept mutate when it enters into the sphere of religious ideology? After all, ideological groups cannot gain strength in numbers if they cannot make a promise of deliverance. As I struggled to find some plausible explanations for this dangerous mutation, my mind travelled back to a very profound lesson given by my father and I must situate this episode within a proper framework.

My father was a Manager in bank and for considerable number of years in his career an active union leader. His bookshelf was stacked with writings of Karl Marx and other leftist intellects, and they existed alongside his other passion – books on spirituality, music and literature. Marx did not necessarily clash with Saint Tyagaraja and each had his own place in his life. He had a firm belief in the role of banks in the society – to uplift the poor and create possibilities for economic growth and achieve social justice. His idealism was not necessarily rewarded, often clashing both with the management and the labor force. My father was a very well read man, his ideas well thought out, to which he was firmly committed. It was this trait in him that was annoying to his higher-ups. He also had a very strong work ethic and insisted that 'union' was not an excuse to shirk responsibilities which irritated many workers. He did pay a big price in his career with transfer to places that would curtail his activism and I think this stress ultimately led to his premature death due to heart attack.

Now that I look back at his life, particularly few years before his demise, I realise that he recognised deep irony in activism and the price that one must pay for it. It was during this intensely contemplative period in his life that I turned eighteen and on my birthday he handed me his copy of *The Second Sex* by Simone de Beauvoir. I was taken aback by the title. He pointed to the subtitle 'The classic manifesto of the liberated woman' and said,

"Now that you are a grown up, it is time to read some liberation philosophies. Read them thoroughly and put them to practice, but learn to take a critical look at them before you become their prisoner".

At that time I found these remarks to be cryptic, but his anguished tone encoded these words permanently in my memory.

Today I am an academic teaching Marx, de Beauvoir and in my private life a woman of faith. My father's words still ring in my ears and I realise how valuable this lesson has been. I have read the works of many leftist intellects and visited several former communist nations on academic projects. I have come to appreciate the most compelling arguments that this philosophy has produced. I have also seen and read self-proclaimed 'Marxists' who have taken ideas completely out of context or twisted ideas to an unrecognisable level. Worse still are the innumerable number of cadres all over the world who claim that they are 'revolutionaries' committed to social change and are ardent worshippers of Marx, but have never read a sentence written by him. And of course all of us have seen the collapse of Marx's Communist Manifesto. The trend is no different in feminism. The most exciting chapter in my graduate study was in feminist scholarship. While I continue to teach it with great passion, I recognise that some works are dated and some are shallow and some are outright useless and dangerous. In the realm of faith, the whole world has seen how fundamentalists have hijacked religion. My wise father was right; every '-ism' has many '-ists' who are either wedded to a phantom idea that cannot make contact with the changing world or stubbornly hold on to it and even resort to violence to enforce it. When you recognise that you are about to become a prisoner of your own liberation philosophy, it is time to take a critical look, or even worse is when liberation ideologies are instruments of deception, exploitation and justification for violence, it is time to resist and challenge.

Interestingly, ancient texts have not only authorised a good challenge to religious institutions, but also deemed it necessary to achieve a superior degree of spirituality. According to *Natya Sastra*, when Sage Bharata's sons were despatched to earth to teach dramatic art forms they brought along *Vidusaka*—the ritual clown who plays the role of the *Sutradhar*—the storyteller in the drama. As a storyteller-cum-commentator and satirist his role is to connect the exalted to the ordinary, art to life, heaven to earth and gods to humans and to achieve this he freely uses comedy and bawdy language. Appearing to be a gluttonous buffoon, he tosses words, juggles concepts, twists meanings and utters profanities fearlessly on all revered entities. He is the satirist who exposes hidden meanings and he is also the apotropaic priest who guards the most sanctified form of the religion and hence his role is protected by the *Omkara*—the mystic monosyllable that encompasses creation, sustenance and dissolution. As a link between myth and reality, stage and audience, his task is to keep the system open-ended so that philosophical doctrines respond to earthly conditions. But there is a built-in danger in this necessary connection; it can be easily abused. Most violations on human dignity and freedom occur under the official banner and most uncivilised acts are committed in the name of god under the pretext of maintaining civility in the society. The *Vidusaka* is forever vigilant about such matters; it is his task to peel various layers of hypocrisies and add layers of meanings. Without the vigilance of the *Vidusaka*, sanctimoniousness passes off as sanctity and hypocrisy passes off as piety.

There seems to be a built-in paradox in all entities ranging from religion to social structure to even raw nature. I have been pondering about 'height' as an image and a concept, and reaching great 'heights' seems to be a two faced; it is at once thrilling and terrifying, indicator of success and yet an inhibitor of growth. There is deep irony to heights in every realm, be it physical or social and a wonderful poem "*Never Place Me So High*" by Atal Bihari Vajpayee, who incidentally was the former Prime Minister of India, comes to my mind. About the sheer physical aspect, the Poet Statesman writes:

> On a very high mountain
> Trees cannot take root,
> Plants do not grow,
> Grass will not survive.

The mountain heights can be a residing place only for God, but for the rest of mortal beings it is "cold as death" and "whose touch alone turns water to stone" as the poet says and therefore, "no sparrow can build a nest there, nor a tired traveller rest even for a moment in its shadow". This principle holds well on the social plane also and in Vajpayee's words "to stand apart without a context" and "severed from one's own" is to live like a "lone hermit in a void" and bear the burden alone. Isolation is not a virtue in the earthly life and Vajpayee asserts:

To be lost in the crowd,
To be immersed in remembrance,
To forget oneself,
Gives fragrance to life,
A meaning to existence.

In the earthly life every entity needs other entities to fully reveal the depth of a possible range of meanings. I can see myself only through the eyes of the other; the others may not necessarily complete me, but they certainly expose my incompleteness. The culture that I embody also reveals itself fully and profoundly when encountering other cultures and when my faith comes in contact with other faiths it shows multiple paths in the spiritual journey. It is an epistemological reality and a creative necessity. To disregard this fundamental principle is to dwell in false consciousness and ugly chauvinism and so I appeal to that Lord of High Mountains in poet Vajpayee's words:

My Lord!
Never place me so high,
That I cannot embrace
Those who are not my own.

(*Unchaai* – Never Place Me So High,
by Atal Bihari Vajpayee)

The journey to Kailash made me realise in the most profound and intimate manner that Creation is the harmony of contrary forces which give rhythm to the Cosmic Dance and melody to Divine Music. This cosmic symphony gently pushed away the restlessness within me caused by nagging questions about my life, my world and my self. But then the post-pilgrimage life brought unprecedented chaos and terror at a global level and the contrary forces don't seem to be in harmony. The indications are not all that optimistic in the current social and political climate. It is difficult to escape the mass paranoia created in political discourses about an elusive enemy and it is equally difficult to ignore suicidal explosions. Political action seems to be ineffective and political discourses are inarticulate. Two ongoing conflicts and trends cause deep disgust and anger within me and they attack my identity to the core: one, as a citizen of The United States of America about the invasion of Iraq and the other as a Hindu about rising Hindu fundamentalism in India.

A war with no achievable goal and no identifiable enemy and no exit plan is inherently pathological. Politicians may mask the cries of the wounded with words of glory, honour and patriotism and use it as a platform to win elections, but the vanquished know the essence of war. Young men and women who cannot look forward to anything more than a minimum wage job are enticed to join the Marines to embody "Honour, Courage and Commitment", so that they can receive educational benefits. As a faculty at a public university – The City University of New York, I routinely see many such young men in my classrooms who have served and are likely to serve again in Iraq and their tales don't necessarily sing the glory of liberty and freedom. They have been too close to the mangled bodies and suicidal explosions. They may have difficulty understanding dialectical idealism and dialectical materialism in my classroom, but they certainly know that ideals quickly vanish and material goods recklessly destroyed in a war. They know all too well the perverse necrophilia of the war. There seems to be no end in sight and George W. Bush has declared to the rest of the world in absolute dualistic terms, "You are with us or against us", eliminating all ambiguities, negotiations and alternatives. I do not know how history will judge the war or what kind of history the war will make, but in the meantime hope is supplanted by horror.

In the land of my birth, the most disturbing trend is the rise of Hindu fundamentalism and the periodic sectarian violence. The riots of Gujarat in 2002 were the worst kind of retaliatory action taken by the Hindutva brigade on innocent Muslims. This political movement is a disgrace to Hindus and Hinduism, and they have been shameless and ruthless in exploiting religious icons and symbols, and have been supplying their street soldiers with tridents. In the hands of Lord Shiva the *Trishul*, the trident represents mastery over three worlds and a reminder that he is beyond three aspects of time— past, present and future. It also represents three activities of the Divine Being—Creation, Protection and Dissolution. In the hands of Hindutva cadets the trident is no more than a murderous weapon with a bunch of thugs on a wild rampage.

The rise of religious fundamentalism in many parts of the world is as disturbing as the cold rigidity in another part of the world where religious freedom is restricted and that brings me back full circle to the site of my pilgrimage. The control over Tibet by China is absolute: their religious freedom is restricted, their spiritual practice mocked, their cultural heritage berated, their environment polluted, their writers persecuted and their monks continue to be tortured. I recently traveled to many parts of China as a Fulbright Scholar and I am convinced more than ever that Tibet is in a no-win situation while China is in a win-win situation. I found it shocking that Tibet was not even an issue, even among the intellects; they think feeble noises are made elsewhere in the world that can be conveniently ignored. In general, the Chinese themselves do not enjoy free press or academic liberty. It was once clamped in the name of Communism and now in the interest of Capitalism. But the greater danger lies in the fact that the world that once was critical, today defers to the Chinese commerce. This is the power of capitalist dictatorship.

But, there is no power on earth that can rob the individuals of their deep feeling for faith—an actual living engagement with their sense of the Divine. Blind belief systems may not stand the test of time or they may become rigid. Religious leaders may fall short or mislead their followers. Religion may be thoroughly misused in the political arena or religious practices may be restricted. But faith that grows and develops with life cannot diminish. It makes no sense to have had the privilege to go to Kailash and see absolute Beauty, hear intense Silence, feel vibrations of a higher Power, taste the Elixir of Life in the waters of the heavenly Lake and hear the mystical Sounds amplified by the winds and return to the world to slip into cynicism. Kailash is a magical place, but I do not want to locate it in the 'dream space' in my consciousness. Each day as I contemplate about my pilgrimage amidst all the chaos in the world, I realise that I need Kailash not because I want to escape from a troubled world, but because I need to actively live in a troubled world.

The fretful cares of everyday life is no match to the great Himalayan wonder. Its grand Nature is too exalted and too high flown in every sense of the expression, and daily life is too ordinary and too humble. But these two worlds must and do merge within me, not as separate entities or as an amalgamated undifferentiated whole, but as partners in a meaningful dialogue questioning and answering each other. I cannot leave what has been experienced in the vastness of space and understood in a much-sought out pilgrimage in the realm of dream or magic and let them remain ineffectual in my life. The wonder that is Kailash comes face to face with my humble prose of life. Life poses questions in varying tones; it pleads, demands, dares, protests and the Silence recorded deep in my soul on the Tibetan plateau responds in varying tones; it calms, suggests, comforts and shows the way. In the journey of my soul, I don't know after how many more births, but at some point in the Grand Time it will dissolve into the Universal Being, but for now I cherish the dialogue. No earthly power can intrude into the private chat room and at no point in time does the dialogic partner refuse to enter into a conversation. This is the Grace of Kailash.

It is not possible to return from Kailash unaffected, nor will its impact fade with time. No one returns empty-handed from the headquarters of the Universal Parents. My fellow pilgrim Shree said that the pilgrimage was a realization of a devotional song that she has been singing since childhood. Another fellow pilgrim Hira said that she realised the grace of her spiritual teacher in the pilgrimage. The inexhaustible mountain stream of Kailash flows through the variegated landscape of life and the parched land must only readily absorb the precious waters. This mighty stream embodies spiritual experiences of countless generations of devotees, singers and dancers, thinkers and poets and infused with so much art and wisdom it is guaranteed to enrich life. The same stream may have different appeal as one matures, but its magic will always endure.

The pictures of Kailash hung on my wall respond to my needs, no matter what the hour is and what my mood is like. When I am calm it shows its sublime beauty, when I am agitated it pacifies me, when I am thrilled it glows and when I am sad it consoles me. It is a wonderful reminder that in this ephemeral world there are some things that stand the test of time. The much-adored Mother Kali of Sri Ramakrishna Paramhamsa will continue to dance on the grounds of death only to bring new life. The Supra Cosmic Being of Sri Aurobindo's philosophical ruminations will continue to descend to earth and make the life Divine. The benevolent Rama of Tyagaraja will appear wherever and whenever there is music with devotion. The young Krishna of Sant Surdas will continue to be mischievous and endear our hearts. The handsome Giridhar of Meera's longing will continue to play the flute much to our delight. The Lord of Dance will continue to depict all the wondrous forms of the Universe. The gods of the unsung heroes and the unheard devotees will prevail. The Lord of Kailash will continue to be my father/Father. This is the dance of the soul and these are my *Movements with the Cosmic Dancer...*

GLOSSARY

✢

The meanings of most Sanskrit words are multi-layered and they signify a very complex range of philosophical concepts. The following meanings are only a simple guide to the reader who may not be familiar with these concepts.

Advaita: The philosophy of Non-Dualism.
Brahman: The Ultimate Reality.
Dharma: Literally 'what holds together' be it social or religious. Broadly it means Duty.
Darshan: To have sight of, especially of a holy symbol or a person.
Gompa: A Buddhist Monastery.
Jivatma: The Individual Self
Karma: The accumulated effect of deeds in lives past and present.
Kismet: A Hindi / Urdu word meaning fate.
Kora: Tibetan word for circling a divine symbol.
Lila: The Cosmic Play
Moksham: Release from the cycle of birth and death.
Mukti: Liberation
Om/Omkara: The mystical monosyllable – The Primeval Word.
Paramatma: The Supreme Self

Parikrama: Religious circumambulation.
Prakriti: Primeval Nature.
Prasad: Sacred offering.
Purusha: Spirit, Individual Soul.
Yatra: Pilgrimage.

OTHER WORKS ON
KAILASH – MANASAROVAR

CLASSIC WORKS

Swami Pranavananda'a *Kailas-Manasarovar*, (published in 1949) to this day remains to be the most comprehensive account, with detailed description of the region woven with spiritual insights. This book is out of print, but with great deal of effort one might find a used copy. Pandit Jawaharlal Nehru wrote the foreword for this book. Swami Pranavananda's other book *Exploration in Tibet* published in 1950 is also a detailed account of the Tibetan region, religion and culture and this is also out of print. Library is the best bet for these books.

The best spiritual account is by Lama Anagarika Govinda in *The Way of the White Clouds: a Buddhist Pilgrim in Tibet*, published by Shambala Publications, Inc., in 1970. This is also out of print. An excellent book and a must read for anybody interested in the spirituality of the region.

The great epic poem is by the Tibetan Saint – Milarepa whose songs are recorded in the Two-Volume book *The Hundred Thousand Songs of Milarepa*, published by Shambala Publications and they are probably available through other publishers as well. It is an epic work for the poet/wanderer in you.

Kalidasa's *Kumarasambhava* and *Meghduta* need no introduction and they take you into the mythical world of Kailash.

Other spiritual accounts include *Wanderings in the Himalayas* by Swami Tapovanam, who was the Guru of Swami Chinmayananda and this book is available from Chinmaya Trust Publications.

Swami Satchidananda's *Kailash Journal* is also an interesting account. This book may be available at any Divine Life Society bookstore.

WESTERN EXPLORERS

Some of the classic works of early western explorers are not available, but one may find them in a library or used books store. They include:

- Ippolito Desideri's *An Account of Tibet* is a fascinating narrative of an early explorer.

- Sven Hedin's three-volume masterpiece *Trans Himalaya: Discoveries and Adventures in Tibet* are highly informative, although some of his geographical claims have been contested and corrected by Swami Pranavananda.

- Sir Francis Younghusband's *Wonders of the Himalayas* published in 1924 is also an interesting book.

CONTEMPORARY WORKS

A great pictorial book with excellent narrative is by Russell Johnson and Kerry Moran in *Tibet's Sacred Mountain: The Extraordinary Pilgrimage to Mount Kailas*, published in 1989 by Park Street Press, Rochester, Vermont in the United States.

Another book with beautiful pictures and spiritual account is by Swami Bikash Giri in *Sumeru Parvat: 12 years of Kailash Manasarovar Pilgrimage and Transformation*. This book is available in English and Hindi and is published by Kailash Ashram. Email: <u>kailasmanasarovar@usa.net</u> for inquiries.

An adventurous account made on foot across Tibet is by Wendy Teasdill in *Walking to the Mountain: A Pilgrimage to Tibet's Holy Mount Kailash*, published by Asia2000 Ltd., in 1996. This book is also out of print, but an excellent tale and one of my favorites.

Other contemporary works include *Circling the Sacred Mountain: A Spiritual Adventure through the Himalayas* by the well-known scholar of Buddhism - Robert Thurman and his student Tad Wise published by Bantam Books in 1999.

In Quest of God: A Pilgrimage to Kailas Manasarovar by Monisha and Nitish Bharadwaj published by India Book House in 2002 is also an interesting book with great photographs.

Kailash Mansarovar: Diary of a Pilgrim by Nilesh D Nathwani published by New Age Books, New Delhi. "Essentially it is an odyssey of spiritual wanderings intermingled with geography, history, tradition and an enduring sense of faith and belief... A highly recommended reading for potential travellers and even for arm-chair pilgrims who will be inspired by its evocatively devotional content."

The Sacred Mountain: The Complete Guide to Tibet's Mount Kailas by John Snelling published by Motilal Banarsidass, Delhi. "What lies ahead of the reader is a kind of literary pilgrimage to the sacred mountain, mainly conducted through an investigation of what was arguably the greatest of them all, Mount Kailash, in well-chosen words and magnificent pictures. It is replete with adventure, and many curious and absorbing things besides."

BOOKS OF RELATED INTEREST

THE BOOK OF HINDU IMAGERY

God's Manifestations and Their Meaning

Eva Rudy Jansen

ISBN: 81-7822-056-3

NOBODY HOME

From Belief to Clarity

Jan Kersschot

ISBN: 81-7822-192-6

EIGHT STEPS TO HAPPINESS

The Buddhist Way of Loving Kindness

Geshe Kelsang Gyatso

ISBN: 81-7822-068-7

BHAGAVAD-GITA

Combined with his Essays on the Gita

William Quan Judge

ISBN: 81-7822-096-2

KAILASH MANSAROVAR

Nilesh D. Nathwani

ISBN: 81-7822-054-7

SOUL POWER

The Transformation that Happens When You Know

Nikki De Carteret

ISBN: 81-7822-145-4

THE HINDU MIND

Fundamentals of Hindu Religion and Philosophy for All Ages

Bansi Pandit

ISBN: 81-7822-007-5

ISLAM

An Historical Introduction

Gerhard Endress

ISBN: 81-7822-156-x

INTRODUCTION TO BUDDHISM

An Explanation of the Buddhist Way of Life

Geshe Kelsang Gyatso

ISBN: 81-7822-065-2